THE MOON ZONE

THE SECOND STEP TO DIVINE PROVIDENCE

NENAD DJORDJEVIC TALERMAN
KADILIYA AILI

Copyright © 2022 Nenad Djordjevic Talerman & Kadiliya Aili

All rights reserved. This book or any portion thereof may not be reproduced or used in any manner whatsoever without the express written permission of the publisher except for the use of brief quotations in a book review or scholarly journal.

Published by Falcon Books Publishing Ltd
Cover design and illustrations by Tanya Robinson
Edited by Maxwell Lewis Latham
First Printing: 2021
Printed in the UK

FALCON BOOKS PUBLISHING LTD
St Neots Masonic Hall
166 School Lane, Eaton Socon
Saint Neots
England
PE19 8EH

www.falconbookspublishing.com
Copyright © 2022
All rights reserved.

ISBN - 13:9780995769243

Ordering Information:
Paperback copies are available on the Falcon Books Publishing website:
www.falconbookspublishing.com

TITLES BY THE AUTHOR(S)

360 Heads of the Earth Zone, The First Step to Divine Providence, Volume I: SPRING, Nenad Djordjevic Talerman. (2021).

360 Heads of the Earth Zone, The First Step to Divine Providence, Volume II: SUMMER, Nenad Djordjevic Talerman. (2022).

Forthcoming Titles

360 Heads of the Earth Zone, The First Step to Divine Providence, Volume III: AUTUMN, Nenad Djordjevic Talerman.

360 Heads of the Earth Zone, The First Step to Divine Providence, Volume IV: WINTER, Nenad Djordjevic Talerman.

The Mercury Zone Shemhamphorash Magic, The Third Step to Divine Providence, Nenad Djordjevic Talerman.

ACKNOWLEDGMENTS

Kadiliya (Isis) and I shared our experiences about the Moon Zone in the magical online forum, 'Studio Arcanis,' starting on the 20th of June 2016.

We planned to dedicate approximately a day to explore every Lunar mansion and its relevant angel over the 28th-day period. Because we thought that 28 days in a row may be too intense, we also consider the possibility of dedicating every Monday to investigating the mansions for 28 consecutive weeks instead. Finally, we chose the first option, even though it seemed to be more demanding. In both cases, discipline had to be strong to accomplish performing the evocations of all the 28 heads of the Moon Zone.

All the members of the forum were invited to participate, but only one member, Moonlit Hermit decided to join our team. He left valuable information about his own experiences on Studio Arcanis, which for the most part matched our own.

I had the great pleasure to meet Isis in Shanghai in August 2016. We spent a brief but unforgettable time together. I was astonished by Isis's personal and spiritual gifts. I do not think that I exaggerate when I say that her communion with the spirits is as easy as people's communication with each other. During this meeting, Isis and I agreed to write this book together about Moon Magic.

I would like to thank Moonlit Hermit for taking part in this magical experiment at Studio Arcanis. Who has over the years inspired my magical path. This list of my friends from Studio Arcanis is very long. As I would not like to mention some while leaving others out. I would like to take this opportunity to offer my gratitude to all of the members with whom I have been in contact and shared friendships and experiences over the past 10 years. Nevertheless, I need to mention. Gilberto. I thank him for all the great fun times and words of wisdom he shared, in the hope that we will make our idea about the Old Viking Club on some tropical island happen in the coming years.

I am also blessed to have become friends with Tanya Robinson, owner and co-founder of Falcon Books Publishing Ltd. In a very short time, Tanya has managed to assemble some of the most important contemporary magicians who also happen to be followers of the great Czech adept Franz Bardon.

CONTENTS PAGE

TITLES BY THE AUTHOR(S) iii
ACKNOWLEDGMENTS v
CONTENTS PAGE vii
FOREWORD..ix
INTRODUCTION xi
THE SECOND STEP TO DIVINE PROVIDENCE................xv
1ST GENIUS – EBVAP 1
2ND GENIUS – EMTIRCHEYUD 9
3RD GENIUS – EZHESEKIS...23
4TH GENIUS – EMVATIBE 29
5TH GENIUS – AMZHERE 35
6TH GENIUS – ENCHEDE 41
7TH GENIUS – EMRUDUE 49
8TH GENIUS – ENEYE..53
9TH GENIUS – EMZHEBYP..57
10TH GENIUS – EMNYMAR 61
11TH GENIUS – EBVEP 68
12TH GENIUS – EMKEPBE 74
13TH GENIUS – EMCHEBA 79
14TH GENIUS – EZHOBAR 85
15TH GENIUS – EMNEPE 95
16TH GENIUS – ECHOTASA 105
17TH GENIUS – EMZHOM..115

18TH GENIUS – EMZHIT 124

19TH GENIUS – EMZHEME 130

20TH GENIUS – ETSACHEYE 138

21ST GENIUS – ETAMREZH 146

22ND GENIUS – RIVATIM 153

23RD GENIUS – LITEVICHE 163

24TH GENIUS – ZHEVEKIYEV 167

25TH GENIUS – LAVEMEZHU 174

26TH GENIUS – EMPEBYN 181

27TH GENIUS – EMZHABE 189

28TH GENIUS – EMZHER 198

FOREWORD

This book is a follow-up to my first book series *360 Heads of the Earth Zone Volumes I-IV-The First Step to Divine Providence*. It should hopefully be helpful for the reader to better understand the following:

- Yesod from the magical point of view
- The Moon's rhythms, phases and cycles
- Moon Magic
- Analogies between the Moon and Lunar colours, oils plants stones and animals
- Analogies between the Moon and tarot
- Lunar concepts and phenomena (foundation, astral illusions, the water of Yesod, dreams, imagination and fantasy)
- Shaddai El Chai

This book also includes the following topics:

- Lunar people and civilizations
- The different planes of the Moon
- Lunar angels and different Lunar angelic orders
- Greek, Roman, and Egyptian Moon gods and Lunar deities in other traditions.
- Lunar astrology
- The functions of the 28 Lunar mansions from a magical viewpoint

This book can provide a chance for a magician to be:

- Initiated into the Moon Zone
- Trained to travel to the Moon and to experience astral and mental wandering around the Moon Zone.
- Successful at evacuating the Archangel Gabriel and other Lunar Spirits

INTRODUCTION

The concept of 28 or (29) Lunar mansions was used since ancient times by the Babylonians, Egyptians, Indians, Chinese, Greeks and Arabians as part of their astrological and calendric system. This system was also adopted by a few notable medieval Arabic and European magicians who argued that the 28 mansions of the Moon were governed by their 28 related Lunar spirits. Those spirits were called 'heads' by the Arabic the Picatrix, while in the European magical tradition (Agrippa, Lemegeton, Solomon's books, Liber Juratus, including Moses' books and F.Barrett) regarded them as 'angels'. Franz Bardon called them 'heads' in the manner they had been regarded by the Arabian medieval magicians.

'Picatrix', (the name of a book and also the pseudonym of its author) argued that each of the 28 Lunar heads exerted both positive and negative influences over our planet. Picatrix instructed the magician how to make proper amulets and effective talismans to evoke each one of the 28 spirits.

The Picatrix, was probably written in the middle of the 11th Century and originally translated into Spanish and then into Latin during the 13th Century. This masterpiece of Arabian magical literature strongly enriched European magical heritage. Medieval European magical view of Lunar magic was highly influenced by this book. Following the same pattern, European magicians named most of the 28 Lunar angels after their related Arabian names from The Picatrix.

Arabian and European magicians argued about the very same Lunar spirits which spread both good and evil influences. For example, Tagriel destroys buildings but also makes people live in love and unity. Bathnael watches over safe trips but also influences divorces in married couples. Egibiel heals people but also can be vengeful and wrathful. Barbiel is an angel with seemingly no Barbiel is an angel with seemingly no positive characteristics at all, while on the other side, Adriel appears with no negative connotations.

The medieval magical concept of one and the same angels being both good and evil can easily confuse the minds of modern magicians. The medieval magicians ascribed to the 28 angels of the Moon so many different and antagonistic functions, that today one cannot be possibly certain which of them could be perceived as good and which of them are not.

Franz Bardon rejected the above-mentioned medieval concept, arguing instead that good spirits do not spread unfavourable and negative influences and that their actions are always good. According to Franz Bardon, bad influences are spread by counter-genii of the good spirits. He emphasized that each of the 28 heads of the Moon zone has his counter-genius. They can be distinguished by observing their influences and actions,

If they spread negative influences, then they are; counter-genii.

Franz Bardon purposely distanced the angels' names from their Arabic and Christianised roots. Even though Bardon did not explain his motivations behind their names' alternation, he quite obviously found it necessary to make a distance from the prior magical paradigm. We may assume that during his numerous experimentations with the Moon magic, Bardon observed that the good angels could not be connected to evil doings. It is also highly probable that the angels themselves dislike when magicians use their names for malevolent purposes. Whatever the reasons, the 28 heads of the Moon Zone appear in Franz Bardon's book under the new names (Emzhabe, Empebyn, Ebvap, Enchede, Lavemezhu etc), while the older names (Adriel, Amutiel, Kyriel, Betnael, Geliel etc) were abandoned.

The lunar angels from the Arabian and Western traditions and the heads of the Moon Zone are the same spirits, even though they now have different names. Emzhabe, the head of the 27th Lunar mansion, confirmed to me that they are the same by handing me a special list of their names and sigils to read, and any magician with a certain experience with the Moon magic may confirm the same.

Franz Bardon refused to give the names and functions of the 28 counter-genii, as he was afraid that some irresponsible magicians could abuse negative lunar forces and knowledge. Nevertheless, if magicians want to satisfy their curiosity about the names of counter-genii, they should start with the source of their original appearance, which is Picatrix.

This book is written as a practical magical guide, with 28 chapters, each of them named after the related head of the lunar mansion.

The chapters consist of the following elements:

- The heads' Arabian and medieval European names;
- The names and the positions of their relevant mansions in the sky and about the Earth Zone.
- Talismans or images and descriptions of their magic, appearances and faculties. Talismans and images which were traditionally used for malevolent purposes are presented in the 'Warning' section of each entry.
- The main characteristics of the counter-genii and their malevolent influences are also observed at the end of each chapter.

Alongside their traditional names, we have also given a modern name to each of the 28 mansions of the Moon. For example, the 1st mansion is traditionally called

Alnath (Horns of Aries), but we also gave it a modern name, "House of Safe beginnings," in the belief that it can be more useful in magical operations.

Each chapter also consists of a short story from my own experiences with the Moon magic, in the hope to encourage the reader's explorations of the Moon zone. The co-author of this book Isis disclosed some of her own remarkable experiences aiming at inspiring the reader to meet some of the most fantastic beings from our part of the universe who inhabit the Moon zone.

Kadiliya and I hope that even a casual reader will find some interesting information about the Moon in this book.

We wish all of our readers to always follow positive vibrations from the Moon.

~Talerman

The Moon Zone

The Second Step to Divine Providence

Nenad Djordjevic Talerman
Kadiliya Aili

1st Genius – Ebvap

Arabian Name: Geriz
Western Tradition: Geniel
Ebvap is the head of the 1st Mansion: Alnath (Horns of Aries)
House of Safe Beginnings: 0°0'0"-12°51'22" Aries
Position of the 1st Mansion in the Moon Zone: Bordering the Earth Zone
Talismans and Images: Traditionally used for malevolent purposes, so they are presented in the 'Warning' section of this entry

Ebvap is an androgyne. Despite traditional descriptions of Ebvap as a man, this spirit may also appear as a woman, or even as a male and female at the same time. This genius is very tall and slim and has an incredibly handsome face. This is an ancient and extremely lucid and powerful intelligence with blonde eyes and dark hair. Ebvap usually wears a long robe which is reflective as a mirror. Ebvap will most probably not appear if you are not good enough at your practical and theoretical knowledge about the Moon magic and evocations. The reason for this is simple. Like so many other spirits, Ebvap dislikes teaching about things which are already available in books.

Ebvap is the main initiator of the Moon magic. This spirit guards all new beginnings, steps and projects, so you may ask

Ebvap for help when you are setting off with something new. Ebvap ignites the initial fire needed for a successful start. If you feel down, you might revive your enthusiasm with Ebvep in the name of Shaddai El Chai! Ebvap can quickly replace potentially malevolent Lunar influences to offer people the following:

- A safe journey,
- A peaceful home,
- A happy family,
- Good friends,
- Good harvest,
- Abundance,
- Success in trade,
- Excellent health,
- Self-confidence,
- Intuition,
- Psychic powers, and
- Understanding of the subconsciousness.

According to the Picatrix (1.4.2), this spirit watches over the safe beginnings of journeys. Ebvap is indeed one of the main guardians of travellers. If you start your journey when the Moon is in Alnath, ask Ebvap to be your guardian! This genius will then make your journey both safe and interesting. It was said that on the day of the 1st Moon Mansion: "The wise men start journeys and take care of their health." If you intend to travel alone, but you are ill, Ebvap will discourage you from travelling and encourage you to stay home and recover instead. If your family members are not comfortable with your journey and are worried about their safety while you are away, Ebvab will also encourage you to postpone your plans until you are all well. With this spirit, your health and security always come first. Ebvap will encourage you to start new projects only when you are at your full strength. This genius also watches over the effective administration of medicines, so you may ask her for help when medicines fail to give results.

Ebvap is also a great spirit to ask for help if you want to initiate into the Tree of Life. You will typically initiate into Malkuth (the Earth Zone) first, and into Yesod (the Moon Zone) second. Nevertheless, Ebvap can help you connect to Archangel Gabriel in order for you to get initiated into the Moon Zone first, if that is your special wish or if you need it. When that happens, Archangel Gabriel and Ebvap can quickly inspire your initiation into the Earth Zone too. Soon after the first evocation of Ebvap, the magician may start exploring the etheric part of the Moon (which in cabala is called Assiah or Expression of Yesod). There might be nothing alive in the physical plane of the Moon, but a part of Ebvap's mission is to demonstrate that the astral dimensions of the Moon Zone are full of life. As far as modern sciences are concerned, the material part of the Moon is not a hospitable region for the maintaining of biological life. Nevertheless, its astral regions offer all possible conditions to support astral life forms which might not be observable by our physical senses but can be reachable through magic.

Ebvap, being one of the great initiators of Lunar astrology, inspired our ancestors to explore the Moon and create the first calendars. Many segments of Lunar astrology are complicated to understand, but after the first successful evocation of Ebvap, you may notice how your capacity of understanding this subject naturally and spontaneously increases.

This is a guardian of many astronomers from both the Moon Zone and the Earth Zone. In this day and age, many astronomers from our world do not see that life might be possible on the Moon and other planets since they search for scientific evidence based on our world's five senses. The root of their scepticism goes back to the old Greek philosopher Anaxagoras who said that everything had a natural explanation, Anaxagoras maintained that Moon was not a living being (Achilles Tatius, *Introduction to Aratus' Phaenomena,* 1.13).

> *........ the Moon is not a god, but a large stone, while the Sun is a hot stone.......*(Plato, Apology, 26d-26e).

Even though modern astronomers tend to reject spirits, Ebvap seems not to mind much about that and will continue to support their studies of the Moon.

Ebvap helps magicians understand tides and electric and magnetic fluids of the Moon. With this genius' help, the magician may become a master of the flows and motions of the Moon. If the Moon stopped influencing the Earth, the blood would stop circulating, rivers would freeze and plants would stop growing, which all would instantly lead to the extinction of life on our planet.

Ebvap is also one of the greatest writers and artists from the Moon Zone. So if you want to write, paint or compose music, you would find in Ebvap one of the best possible teachers.

This spirit may also show you your alternate history and how your probable alternate lives would look like if you made some different decisions in the past.

Ebvap is a great psychopomp too. The 1st Moon Mansion, Alnath, is a huge region. It is the bordering area between the Earth and the Moon, so there you may find many passing, paths, tunnels, bridges and corridors connecting one zone to another.

During your early attempts to reach some higher lunar dimensions, you may end up walking around its lowest astral regions instead. The fog may prevent you from seeing things around you. It can be so dense that it would also sometimes make it difficult for you to walk. A little of what people might manage to spot there would also often be somewhat misshapen. You might also see some spirits there in their etheric forms, but at first, it might not be possible to observe their true figures. It might also be very difficult to get in touch with them, as they often move very fast. You might even spot how some of them are on their quick way down to the Earth for reincarnation or a visit.

It can be very hard to explore those lower planes of the Moon, but if you are truly interested in it, Ebvap may find a proper guide for you from whom you may learn how to do it without having to experience hard times and big difficulties. Once you reach the higher astral regions of the Moon, it will be much easier for you to move around.

You may observe that there are many towns in Alnath. After you reach the higher Lunar ground, you will likely find some spirits nearby. If you are not quite sure where you are, ask them for confirmation that you are on the Moon. Ask them also where to find Ebvap, and they will probably show you the way to that spirit. That being said, once you step on the Moon for the first time, Ebvap may meet you there personally.

Additional Observations Relevant to Ebvap's Teachings on Lower and Higher Moon Regions

The Bulgarian mystic Omraam Mikhaël Aïvanhov advised his students to pass as quickly as possible through the lower plane of the Moon to promptly reach the higher Moon's regions.

Evocation Experiences

Talerman

During this evocation, Ebvap asked me to give him all that I had ever written about the Moon in my lifetime. Suddenly, a few books and a lot of articles about the Moon appeared in my hands, so I handed them all over to him. I was very surprised. Even though those papers seemed to be doubtlessly mine, I was also sure that I had not written them down that way. I had not published any work about the Moon yet, so how could I possibly have all those papers with me? Ebvap explained to me that they were shaped by my thoughts about the Moon and that they were the collection of everything which I had ever said or written online about the Moon. He said he would examine my papers and give his opinion about them later.

A few moments later, I appeared at a school as a teacher. When I looked around the classroom, I saw a few higher selves of my friends. I heard Ebvap telling me that they had little understanding of magic, so he asked me to teach them about the four elements and elemental beings. I am not sure what Ebvap thought about my lecture, because this was also when my session ended.

KADILIYA

The moment I opened my eyes, I seemed to be standing on a bridge. This bridge was white and narrow, but very long. There was nothing underneath me, just air, as it seemed. Above me was the giant Moon. I felt I could almost touch it. The closer I was getting to the Moon, the more clearly I saw a man standing there wearing a long robe. When I arrived, this man came up to me greeting me. I asked if he was Ebvap and he confirmed with a very kind smile. We started walking and I was about to ask him a question, but he spoke first, "Welcome, welcome back."

We came to a tall round building that seemed very old because it was falling apart. There were no doors or windows. Some of its parts seemed to be broken and yet the building looked like it was supposed to be that way. We went inside and I saw some people reading books. It was a giant library. The books were perfectly stacked to the top, but the centre of the building had a hole. Those people who were reading were standing in the air and walking in the air to get to the next book. I honestly did not know what to say, because I was amazed at the architecture of the place and also with how many books were in that space. Ebvap turned to me and said, "That whole section is yours. Thank you for contributing to the selections we have here". I was very confused, so I asked, "What do you mean by contribution?" He replied, "Those books up there in that section are yours. Over many lifetimes you have given us many of your books, findings, understandings and experiences about different realms and dimensions. Here, let me show you." And we walked up to that section. It did not have names or anything, but I felt the vibe like - It's mine but also it isn't. He pulled out a book and opened it. It was an art book. I instantly remembered that piece I had worked on in my dreams. He pulled out another book. There were lots of drawings and writings on it. I asked, "So, some time ago I contributed with my artwork?" And he replied, "Oh yes. In fact many artworks," I continued, "But doesn't this place already have everything you need?" He laughed but did not answer. I looked at a few more books and I recognised my writing and my artwork, and it was real. I just did not know that it had been kept here. It was such a long time ago. He pointed outside for me to look. I turned and looked, but I did not see what he was trying to show me, so he walked with me outside.

  We came to a giant lake which seemed like it went on forever. It reflected tiny silver sparkles. I asked if there was anything I could do for them or if there was anything else they could teach me about, but Ebvap smiled and waved, then slowly disappeared.

Warning

The Picatrix's talisman: A black man with his hair wrapped and in black cloth, standing as a fighter upright on his feet holding in his right hand a lance.
Agrippa's talisman: A black man in a garment made of hair, casting a small lance with his right hand.
Bruno's image: An Ethiopian in an iron chair, belted with a cord, throwing a dart.

Black magic can turn the **House of Safe Beginnings** into the **House of Risky Starts and Disasters.** According to the Picatrix, (4.9,29) the wrathful aspect of Geriz watches over discord between partners. It can also cause servants to flee. Worst of all, it can also cause murders to take place.

An immature magician might get some weird ideas about how to bring destruction to other people with the help of negative Lunar influences from this Mansion.

Life on the Earth is unthinkable without Lunar rays, but to be directly exposed to them while you are exploring their sources on the Moon might be unpleasant and can even physically seriously harm an inexperienced magician. To explore reflections and influences of Lunar forces upon the Earth is one thing, but to have a first-hand experience with them on the Moon is something quite different and it cannot be achieved without proper spiritual guides. Ask for help you with that if you wish to further explore this topic!

2ND GENIUS – EMTIRCHEYUD

Arabian Name: Enedil
Western Tradition: Enediel
The Picatrix's Talisman: A crowned king
Agrippa's Talisman: A crowned king
Bruno's Image: An enthroned king, lifting a prostrated man with his sceptre
Emtircheyud is the head of the 2nd Mansion: Allothaim or Albochan (Stomach of Aries)
The House of Life and Concord: 21°42'12"-25°42'51" Aries
Position of the 2nd Mansion in the Moon Zone: Bordering the Earth Zone

Emtircheyud is one of the mightiest governors of the Moon Zone. This genius often appears as a crowned king wearing a long robe. On less formal occasions, he was also seen in brown clothes wearing a hat with a wide brim. He has very short and straight hair, looks young and is very intelligent. It is most favourable to evoke Emtircheyud during the Waxing Moon because it will be then easier to meet him, especially if you are a beginner.

Emtircheyd teaches about: the Moon's magic, light bodies and souls, agricultural astrology, all phases of the Moon, and mediation. He is also one of the best teachers of the Moon's etheric region. This genius is one of the most important guardians of women (especially if they are pregnant). He also guards the prosperity and concord of people.

Emtircheyud covers most topics about Moon magic. The first Lunar genius Ebvap is the main initiator into the Moon mysteries, so Emtircheyud, as the second Lunar genius, has the mission to teach about the second step in the Moon magic (which covers a lot of different tasks and keys, but most of them are related to the mystery of life).

As the Second Mansion falls during the Waxing or the Full Moon, do not hesitate to ask Emtircheyud to help you with all possible magical things related to the Moon magic, because he covers them all! You may also use this period to achieve astral projection or evoke fairies. They are usually attracted by: carnations, cloves, lavender, chrysanthemum, sunflowers, roses, apples, oaks, and willows. If you are outside at night, Emtircheyud can help you find a fairy circle. When you step inside of it during the Full Moon, your wish might come true. If you believe in witch lore, you may also consider making nine rounds around the fairy circle to make fairies visible.

Among Emtircheyud's many mysteries, life on our planet is at the centre of them all. According to his teachings, biological life had not yet been developed on Earth when the Moon separated from our planet. After the division between them had taken place, the Moon did not develop biological forms of life, but it did help the Earth expand its first life forms based on material, biological and organic existence.

This genius wrote many books about the Moon. One of his most important books is about the 28 Lunar angels. This book has an illustration of him as a mighty king on the cover page. You may certainly read in this book many untold mysteries about the Moon. Agrippa, Bardon, and some other authors were directly inspired by this book while they were writing about the Moon.

According to Franz Bardon, Emtircheyud is responsible for "controlling the rhythm in our physical world". In other words, this genius teaches about how different Lunar rhythms may affect the physical plane and life on our planet. Without the Moon, there would certainly be no life. Archaeological discoveries suggest that people might have been taught how to observe Lunar rhythms and phases 37.000 years ago. The old script also observed that all things which reinforce the blooming of life are always supported by Emtircheyud. As it is written in the medieval "Ashmole 396," when the Moon is in the Second Mansion it is good to sow seeds, but it is not good to plant trees. In the Picatrix, this angel presides over: the digging of successful wells, finding hidden treasures, and planting wheat.

Most magicians agree that prosperity work is another very important field of this genius's influence. The astrologer Alexandre Volguine confirmed in 1974 that it is good to make pentacles for the discovery of springs and treasures when the Moon is in the Second Mansion.

When it comes to the Moon phases, the magician may, for example, ask him why the Moon is more potent as it grows. His answers to that question will most probably surprise you because he knows how to articulate in a way that has never been seen or heard of in our reality on Earth.

All mysteries about the Full Moon may also be revealed by this genius. The Full Moon has traditionally been the best time for Lunar magic especially if the magician wanted to achieve: positive thinking, love, friendship, healing, travelling and abundance. So, if you want to achieve any of these things, Emtircheyud can help. Just remember to conjure him during the Full Moon phase. The main problem with the Full Moon is that it lasts only for 24 hours, thus many magicians use one day before and one day after its appearance in the sky for some magical purposes. Emtircheyud can also help people empower their magic during those three essentially important days.

Many magicians pay special attention to the Moon's Waning phases because they might be at their most vulnerable state to black magic activities. In this phase, you may ask

Emtircheyud to banish all bad demons from your life, reject all evil influences and remove: illnesses, bad habits, negative thought patterns, jealousy and envy. Picture the Moon taking everything negative away with itself while it is waning! Be confident, once the Moon disappears from the sky, all negative influences will also vanish with it too. As the master of the Lunar phases and rhythms, Emtircheyud has many original stories to tell about the Waning Moon and how it is seen from different traditions all around the world.

In his Lunar region, you may find a lot of guardians of life. They are connected to everything that grows and multiplies on our Earth. Those rigorous energy workers take their job very seriously as all life on the Earth depends partly on them. Part of their job is to transfer solar and other cosmic energies towards the Earth to make life possible on our planet. Those spirits are not only ready to demonstrate to us how they do it, but they can also tune us into some very specific Lunar flows to make us masters of life as well. Emtircheyud is directly ruled by the Divine name of Shaddai El Chai. He may teach the magician how to transform all manifestations of upper spheres into life forms, as they descend towards the Earth.

Emtircheyud often encourages people to treat everyone (especially women) with respect. This angel can help you have good relations with your: wife, girlfriend, female friends and female members of your family. Ask Emtircheyud for help if you see a female friend having issues with her mental health or suffering from menstrual problems and hysteria. Evoke Emtircheyud, wear his sigil and carefully listen to his instructions on how you may heal or help your female friends.

In many languages, words for the Moon and menstruation are similar and in some cases identical. Ask Emtircheyud to explain why the 9 months of pregnancy are linked to the Moon and the number 9! As he is the best expert on life in the Moon Zone, his answers may surprise you, especially because he would not tell you about things which have already been written in books from our world's reality.

This gentle angel encourages magicians to remove hate from their own and other people's hearts. Magicians from the past already experienced this angel's role in removing anger and inspiring reconciliation. According to the Picatrix, reconciliation is the main point why this angel was conjured in the first place: "Thou, O Enedil, drive away this anger with NN from me, and let me be reconciled with him, and let my petition be agreeable to him." Related to this angel's talisman, the Picatrix has pointed out that it should be used against the wrath of very important persons. Emtircheyud certainly inspires magicians to make peace with their superiors, avoid arguments, and be in harmony with other people, friends and family members. His role in maintaining good relations with superiors has been especially noted, so if you happen to argue with your bosses, ask this angel for help. He may even help you become a spiritual teacher to your superiors if that is your wish. Additionally, Emtircheyud may also assist you to be on friendly terms with dignitaries (presidents, kings, prime ministers, etc.), if you are in their service. According to the contemporary astrologer Christopher Warnock, the Second Lunar Mansion "foretells a positive resolution to the conflict" and "can also indicate that this is a good time to seek a favour, particularly from one in a position of "authority". This astrologer also suggests that when the Moon is in the Second Mansion the "time may be ripe for asking an employer for a raise, or seeking a favourable ruling from a judge."

This genius can also offer his assistance as a psychopomp and guide the magician anywhere around the Moon Zone. He can also send you back in time allowing you to revisit your past. Emtircheyud's region is one of the most intense and mystical parts of the Moon. It is very dynamic and yet balanced, as it is in perfect equilibrium with all other Sephirot on the Tree of Life. This part of the Moon receives subtle yet powerful and creative energies from Kether via Tipharet (the Sun Zone on the Tree of Life), which then gets transferred down to the Earth Zone into our material world. On the Moon, Emtircheyud oversees the vital importance of flora and fauna of our Earth since from his regions the activation of the whole organic life takes place to create the Earth's biosphere.

Franz Bardon has said that Emtircheyud cooperates with some heads of the Earth Zone in controlling the rhythm of our physical world. He did not mention the names of the heads he had in mind, but according to our research, they ought to be: Kiliki, Opollogon and Ramage. The first three Lunar Mansions bordering the Earth Zone, from our planet's side, belong to the three named heads. In those bordering regions, magicians may learn everything they might like to know about the creation of life on our planet and the etheric connections between the Moon and the Earth Zone. Many spirits from those areas can teach you about the importance of the ether for life. So they teach about the Hindu principle of prana (life energy that penetrates all nature and living beings) and Chinese Qi (vital energy and cosmic spirit that penetrates and brings life to all things). Ask them to elaborate on any question you might wish to know about the origin and purpose of life! If you want to start practising the Moon magic, Kiliki is one of the best spirits from the Earth Zone to ask for help. Opollogon's region is one of the largest bordering territories between the Earth and Moon zones and is very moon-like. In Opollogon's temples, you might see priests from both the Earth and the Moon performing together Divine Liturgy on 7° Aries and some other special dates and festivals. Ramage's region looks more like it is located on the Moon than on Earth. The sky is their silvery-dark and Lunar symbols can be seen everywhere.

Emtircheyud can also help you create a peaceful place for your study, even if there is disruption all around you. This genius will not let other people harm your progress. Ask him for help if you find yourself wasting your time on the Internet or paying attention to things which are not of your concern!

Additional Observations Relevant to Emtircheyud's Teachings

Life-Giving Source

Some ancient sages knew that Lunar rhythms regulate: body fluids, tides, rain, fertility, menstrual cycles and the growth of plants. They were aware of the Moon's ability to influence the movements of oceans and human souls alike, and also cause the multiplication of all flora and fauna on the Earth. Among them, Plinius the Elder recognized the Moon as the most essential point of all mundane rhythms, so he called the Moon the "Star of our Lives," and also said that the Moon circulates the blood in our organism.

Pregnancy

Ancient sages knew that the Moon was a source of all fertility on the Earth and that it could also enhance pregnancy. Zohar (III, 296) talking about the Moon, explains: "All laws, all juices, all powers are united here. All powers of existence pass through this point through the organs of reproduction." Even though today it is mostly seen as a superstition, women from the past were much motivated to sleep under the moonlight when they wanted to have children, so they also used to cover themselves with pearls and shells for that purpose too.

Waxing Moon

Old sages observed that the Waxing Moon attracts abundance, so they used that time to focus on beginnings, new enterprises and good luck. They also used this phase to cut their hair. Old Egyptians bowed three times at the appearance of the Waxing Moon in the sky referring to Osiris, Isis and Horus. Some people still make a wish by turning a silver coin around their pockets or inside their wallets when they see the Waxing Moon. When it appears on Monday, it brings good luck and good weather. The Solomon Key points out that the magician should evoke when the Moon is 2, 4, 6, 8, 10, 12 or 14 days old; while the other days are not beneficial for evocation. The 6th day of the Waxing Moon was important for druids too. Angels appeared to Abraham on the 4th day of the Waxing Moon. Slavic nymphs like to dance during the Waxing Moon, but their laughter may disturb men's minds. The Waxing Moon is very significant for all of the magician's magical work of materialization and manifestations. The magician should avoid pointing out the Waxing Moon standing in front of the window or through the tree crowns as it might not be a beneficial omen. The Waxing Moon announces 20 days of rain and wind when it appears on Saturday and it predicts flood until the end of the month when it appears on Sunday.

Full Moon

- Holi was celebrated in India for two days, in March, with dancing and singing. Indian sages honoured the Full Moon as a protector of their cows. When Krishna appears in the forest during the Full Moon, his devotees (the gopi) would leave their jobs, family, homes and physical bodies to join him in dance and play.
- Theravada Buddhists celebrate the Full Moon once a year, in April or in May, when they observe important events from the Buddha's life.
- Chinese ghost festival (guijie) is celebrated all over East Asia during the 7th lunar calendar.

- Eliphas Levi writes in "History of Magic" that the magician might prepare his elixir of life if he withdraws from the world in May during the Full Moon. He should then stay in nature for 40 days drinking the May dew and eating plants.
- Alice Baily was 15 years old when she was invited in 1895 to attend the "Full Moon of May" ceremony in the Himalayas. She had been so fascinated by this experience that she formed her Arcana school which organized group meditations during the Full Moon

Waning Moon

- The old Brits used Ophioglossum lusitanicum during the Waning Moon because they believed that its substance could remove snake poison.
- Witches from Europe and America used chrysanthemums as they believed that this plant could remove evil spells
- If a modern Wicca is attacked during the Waning Moon, she would protect herself with a chrysanthemum or with its core.
- Tibetan Buddhists see the Waning Moon as a period of powerful negative, female and yin phases. The 25th day of the lunar month, "Dakini Day" is connected to the enlightened female energy and some lamas practice it that day.
- In Slavic cultures, it was believed that if a child was born during the Moon's least visible phase, a boy would become the werewolf and a girl the vampire.
- "Zohar" warns that the demon Lilith is especially active during the Waning Moon.

Evocation Experiences

Talerman

As I was failing to evoke some spirits from the Earth Zone, surprisingly enough I heard someone telling me: "Leave the Earth. It is now time for the 2nd Mansion." Soon after I appeared somewhere on the Moon. The black sky was covered by silver cosmic lights. Black mountains had strange oval shapes and some of them looked like pyramids. They covered the landscape all the way long to the horizon. Suddenly, Emtircheyud appeared in front of me as a crowned king from the past centuries. He showed me many different things on the Moon, but first, he sent me back in time so that I could play with my son who was again 1 year old.

This genius also showed me his grimoire about the 28 Lunar angels. He let me read it, but regrettably, I forgot most of it. Hopefully, I kept some things which I read in my subconsciousness. All of a sudden, the book disappeared from my hands, and I heard Emtircheyud asking me if I wanted to join his expedition which was about to explore the Moon Zone. His expedition had many members. I accepted his invitation, but my session was over before we set off.

This genius also likes to organize parties, and another time when I was exploring the Second Mansion, he invited me to be his guest. The party was in a tavern and was very loud. Everybody was drinking, singing and talking loudly, but when they saw me, everyone fell silent. Emtircheyud came up to me to introduce me to his friends, among whom there were a few other heads of the Moon Zone.

KADILIYA

I saw a triangle with a golden spiral inside spinning slowly. I looked at the spiral for a while, but then, not sure why I noticed how I was walking up a spiral staircase. I stopped and looked around. I seemed to be inside a tight tower going up. The walls had a specific golden symbol all over. There was a tall window without glass, so I looked outside. I saw lots of towers but I could not see what was beneath. I started walking up until I reached the top. There was a red door that had "Emtircheyud" written on it in golden letters. I went to knock on but my hand just went through the door. I was puzzled and tried it again and the same thing happened. I stood there a bit, then went inside. Something pulled me a little and I was standing in a round-shaped room.

There were two men, one was sitting on a fancy red chair. He was wearing medieval puffy red clothes. He had curly short hair and a small facial structure. His body was also small. I asked him if he was Emtircheyud and he replied, "No, but he is," and pointed to the man standing next to him. That man was wearing a long beige-colored robe with golden embroidery all over it.

Emtircheyud invited me to go with him and we walked towards a wall which turned into a door. We walked through it and found ourselves standing in space. I told him why I came and he started to talk about the light body, saying that it is another aspect of the soul and that those two are deeply connected. Emtircheyud continued, "The soul has certain attributes and the light body is just one of them. The more you use the light body, the stronger it becomes and eventually, it will wake up. When it wakes up, that is when the real materialization of thoughts and intentions takes place. You can see around some people something which looks like an aura but is slightly denser than that. It is the light body. It provides a layer of space and time. When it is activated, it creates a safe space/time/dimension that can be used for personal space detachment from everything and everyone or for a specific purpose. Think of it as an office space. For whatever purpose you want to use it, it can create for it, while providing the correct feel to it. The light body is made of the same constitution as the soul. It cannot be harmed because it is against the law of time and space. It can be influenced but only if the person allows it. It is also connected to the centre of the heart. The light body can provide space for healing and creativity. If you use the light body more often with awareness and trust, you can awaken it, which also means that it will then become aware of your commands and awareness. Treat your relationship with your light body with respect and trust and learn how to love it". As he went on, I was seeing the light body visually. He recommended using the light body during meditations, any magical work, dream work and for healing. In the end, he said that people know very little about the soul. He was quite enthusiastic about teaching all this to me.

Warning

Black magic can turn the **House of Life and Concord** into the **House of Degenerative Life Forms and Discord.** According to the Picatrix, Enedil's wrathful presides over destroying unfinished buildings, enraging men against each other, and improving the incarceration of slaves. The medieval Ashmole 396 Manuscript has warned that when the Moon is in this Mansion, you should not wed, take new fellowship, buy cows or sheep, plant trees or wear clothes. This manuscript has also underlined, "if you be taken prisoner, you are likely to be long imprisoned." Agrippa and some other medieval sources also agree about how this Mansion is particularly perilous to prisoners. Thus, if they have good reasons for that, magicians may ask this angel to prolong the sentence of prisoners and make their lives in prison as difficult as possible.

All medieval sources also warn that it is perilous to travel on the water when the Moon is in the Second Mansion. The last century astrologer Alexandre Volguine warns people not to travel on the water during that day to prevent painful events such as "death, exile, or bad business dealings." Black magicians can exactly do the opposite to use that day to endanger the lives of their enemies if they travel on water. They may also try to disturb relations among friends and escalate some of their minor misunderstandings into very serious arguments. Maybe the worst what the black magician might be thinking of trying to do is to prevent Lunar life-giving rays from reaching the Earth or even to misshape them to make new creations look unhealthy and degenerative once they manifest upon the Earth.

Many Lunar spirits often operate in the etheric part of the Earth from where they strongly influence our lives, but not all of them are benevolent. Malevolent spirits can escalate minor problems to some massive dimensions, especially when the Moon is in the Second Mansion. The magician who is ready to abuse Emtircheyud's knowledge can create all kinds of problems for other people. In a matter of seconds, the black magician could be able to make an energetic person extraordinarily aggressive or a mildly melancholic person deeply depressive. We can freely say that some Lunar spirits are evil alchemists because they can transform people's patriotism into extreme chauvinism and love for God into religious fanaticism. They can even easily transform love into hate and tranquillity into a rage. If you notice the described tendencies in or around you, ask at once Emtircheyud to banish bad demons that are provoking them.

When the Second Mansion is during the New Moon, some wizards and witches might get tempted to draw dark and demonic powers from the Moon. Some magicians may take advantage of some people who are sensitive to the Full Moon. During the Full Moon phase in the Second Mansion, they may also use this opportunity to cause people temporarily lose their psyches and minds.

If the magicians decide to go along these or similar perilous sideways, they will in all probability end up miserably alone. And there is a saying on the Moon: "The one who abuses the powers of the Moon will also die alone on the Earth and the one who dies alone on the Earth will remain alone on the Moon or anywhere else through all eternity."

3rd Genius – Ezhesekis

Arabian Name: Anuncia or Amixiel
Western Tradition: Anixiel
The Picatrix's Talisman: The figure of a seated woman with her right hand raised over her head
Agrippa's Talisman: A woman sitting in a chair, her right hand lifted up on her head
Bruno's Image: A well-dressed woman, sitting in a chair, with her left hand raised over her head
Ezhesekis is the head of the 3rd Mansion: Alchaomazon or Athoray (Pleiades)
House of Happiness : 25°42'51" Aries - 8°34'17" Taurus
Position of the 3rd Mansion in the Moon Zone: The centre of the Moon Zone
Talismans and Images: Medieval talismans, rightly, depict Ezhesekis as a woman, because she appears either as a beautiful female child or a nurturing mother figure. Actually, she often looks like a Chinese or Japanese girl

Whatever form she takes, she is very active in the physical world. If correctly evoked, she may even emerge in her physical appearance. The best way to connect with her is to be in nature and to contemplate under the moonlight, especially by the sea, river or lake. After the first evocation of Ezhesekis, the magician should be able to spot either her personal or her subordinate spirits clearly anywhere in nature.

She teaches about: freedom, beauty, art, sailing, success and creativity. She is one of the masters of empathy and compassion. If magicians want to help other people with all earthly matters (which are for better or worse usually related to money, love and health), they may do it with Ezhesekis' help. According to the Picatrix, this angel helps with the acquisition of all good things such as to sail and returning safely, completing works of alchemy, finishing all works done by fire, hunting successfully, and causing love between husband and wife. Ezhesekis teaches magicians to open up their imagination, enjoy life and make use of positive Lunar influences for their own earthly happiness.

Agrippa has said that Third Lunar Mansion is profitable to sailors, huntsmen, and alchemists. In the medieval "Ashmole 396 Manuscript" it is written that it is good for commerce. This Mansion has many positive signs according to modern astrologers as well. Christopher Warnock has written that it indicates: wealth, prosperity, career, and "full flowering of art, beauty and creativity". According to Alexandre Volguine, this Mansion provides powerful emotions, determination, and a great capacity for work. Franz Bardon has written that Ezhesekis can teach the magician to "procure for himself, in the Akasha-principle, happiness and everything good", and also "good luck and success in all earthly matters". Ezhesekis will certainly bring happiness to the magician's everyday activities. Her ideal is to see the magician in a state of eternal happiness and satisfaction.

Ezhesekis' region is one of the most pleasant and beautiful parts of the Moon. It is balanced with the Middle Pillar of the Tree of Life, so it is full of happiness which is stable, balanced and firm. It is actually Lunar paradise. Free of worries, spirits can engage fully in spiritual studies and contemplation. They enjoy their existence there to the fullest, though among some of them, there are also some elements of hedonistic activities. Ezhesekis' motto is: Everything is all right, so it is time to relax and enjoy life! She may offer the magician numerous different kinds of meditative techniques just for a purpose of relaxation.

Magicians who closely work with this genius will learn a lot about empathy and compassion. They will open their hearts to all people and will understand that everyone needs some form of help in their lives from time to time. Your happiness, according to this angel, would be totally fulfilled if you manage to find a way how to help people in need. Ezhesekis inspires the magician to help people to achieve success in all of their earthly matters. According to Cynthia Schlosser, Ezhesekis' angels "flood the Earth with flowing tangible feelings in the body of happiness and joy", so that "Heaven can manifest on Earth."

When the Moon is in its 3rd Mansion, it is a good time to: see friends, hike, have a picnic, hunt or play with domestic animals. Ezhesekis likes to see friends join together in different social activities, as she truly enjoys seeing people happy. The magician who has good relations with Ezhesekis will have many opportunities and occasions to celebrate.

Additional Observations Relevant to Ezhesekis' Teaching on Happiness

In Vedic astronomy, the Moon is the key to calculating if one is having a happy life or not. The Moon was to the ancient Indians a symbol of home, mother and a peaceful mind.

Evocation Experiences

Talerman

I saw three young Chinese people at the bus station. They told me that they were heading for a tourist trip to the Shaolin monasteries and later to some other important spiritual places. They asked me to join in. I had to decline them politely as I was at that moment performing ancestral magic and was on my way to see my dead grandparents instead. One of them, a young man, was very sad to hear that I could not go with them. The second girl looked also very sad. I was about to change my mind because of their reactions, but the third girl, who seemed to be the leader, told them not to be sorry and that we would meet another time anyway. She said that she was Ezhesekis and then they went away. I was very surprised because that night I had no intention to evoke her, but she appeared to me anyway.

The next time I saw her, she told me that the easiest way to attract Lunar energies for happiness is by the sense of smell. While she was speaking, she showed me a statue of an elephant, pointing out that it is a great talisman for attracting happiness. She also said that the best magicians are the ones who do their magic with easiness, which is only possible if they are relaxed.

Kadiliya

This was a short vision. I opened my eyes and saw a small Japanese girl sitting in front of me. She was staring at me with her adorable large eyes. She looked very curious and so was I. We both looked at each other for a while. I noticed I was in a Japanese-styled room. She finally got up, grabbed my hand and opened a door. We walked out and then everything went blank.

Warning

Black magic can turn the **House of Happiness** into the **House of Exaggerations.** This could push people towards fornication, immorality, vices and narcotics. Happiness might become a curse. The Picatrix has warned that Annuncia wrathful helps to "more firmly incarcerate captives," with which the "Ashmole 396" also agrees, "If you are arrested, you shall long abide in prison and lose your goods."

Christopher Warnock warns that with this Lunar Mansion there may also be too much of a good thing. His advice is, "We must be careful not to overindulge our appetites, be it literally in eating and drinking or metaphorically, in our desire for the good things of the material world". Luckily, the magician who has good contact with Ezhesekis, will also have many opportunities to enjoy life to the fullest, but without fear of experiencing its side effects caused by exaggerations.

On the other side, Ezhesekis will most probably withdraw her assistance if magicians take their happiness for something granted. If you are never satisfied with what you have and who you are, this genius will not bother to help you.

Counter-effects of magic with Ezhesekis may also make immature people: bored with life, envious, neurotic, and misanthropic

4ᵀᴴ Genius – Emvatibe

Arabian Name: Assarez
Western Tradition: Azariel
Emvatibe is the head of the 4th Mansion: Aldebaram or Aldelamen (Eye or Head of Taurus)
House of Protection: 8°34'17" - 21°25'40" Taurus
Position of the 4th Mansion in the Moon Zone: It consists of two parts, the first being a buffer transit zone with many bridges, walls, stairs, and other traps and hindrances which you should pass through in order to reach its second part which is secretive and paradise-like and where Emvatibe has his headquarters. It is highly unlikely that any demons or unwelcome guests could have a chance to enter this secret part of Emvatibe's Mansion.
Talismans and Images: Traditionally are used for malevolent purposes, so they are presented in the 'Warning' section of this entry

Emvatibe often appears as a knight in silver armour holding a giant sword, but he was also seen wearing a black long coat. He has long straight black hair. He has a peculiar, almost half-female and half-male face. This powerful spirit will teach only the advanced, serious and mature magician. He sometimes promotes his students to the generals of the Moon and then bestows them with enormous magical powers in which they can easily defeat any potential enemies. Franz Bardon explains that such powers, among other things, imply: "Words and formulae for banning which enable the magician to paralyze or even kill a person, or whole groups of persons, at the moment of their utterance". He is a kind but also stoic disciplinarian, highly skilled at all combat arts. Emvatibe is one of the mightiest warriors on the Moon. If you do not have a stronger constitution or a heart of a true warrior, it might not be so easy to evoke him.

A version of his talisman is not by chance shaped as a soldier riding a horse with a snake in his right arm. This snake symbolizes his sword. Emvatibe is closely connected to all mysteries which are related to the sword as a magical weapon. You might be tested by him to use your sword in combat against him. He respects true warriors, thus the magician should be in excellent physical shape and health when they evoke this spirit. Take your sword with you when you evoke this spirit because he will not appreciate it if you do not.

Main Emvatibe's mission is to guard the magician against malevolent people. He is similar to Echotasa, the head of the 16th Mansion. The two of them mostly differ in that Emvatibe usually protects against malevolent people, while Echotasa guards against malevolent spirits. Emvatibe discovers enemies and reveals their secret plans. He also gives instructions on how to protect against all other mean human beings. This genius also reveals secret cliques, societies and cults which have been founded to cause harmful events or situations.

Because Emvatibe removes malevolent, malicious and violent people from your life, with him as your guardian, you may freely walk across the most dangerous parts of town at night without fear of robbery or attack. Anyway, if you happened to be attacked or get into any sort of trouble, remember to evoke Emvatibe and he will find a way how to protect you. He may also remove your troublesome neighbours, fake friends and mischievous colleagues from your life, though that can take some time for him to arrange. Emvatibe helps you defend your individual rights when they are jeopardized by some institutions.

This genius may teach you how to create excellent protective talismans against all maligned people. With Emvatibe as your guardian, you will live and work in safe environments which will also give you a good standard of living and constant opportunities for good results in any important matters.

Emvatibe is one of the most powerful guardians of comradeship in the Moon Zone, so he is also capable of removing all the toxic people in one's life and also in return of providing many positive and trustworthy friends. He is a special protector of business partners who are in any way united to achieve certain common goals. He will certainly help your team win if he finds your goals noble and honest. This genius can also influence other people to do exactly what you want them to do, but you must first explain to him why he would help.

As our time in this incarnation approaches its end, Emvatibe will encourage us to pardon all of our enemies and forgive everybody for everything in order to move on towards new dimensions as blessed souls and free spirits.

Emvatibe is also a great protector against dangerous animals. According to the Picatrix, this angel was called to kill and bind reptiles and venomous animals. Remember to ask him for protection if you are out in the wild and in fear that beasts might attack you, especially if you happened to be at risk of being bitten by a snake!

Additional Observations Relevant to Emvatibe's Teaching on Protection Against Enemies

You may also additionally use the 5th Pentacle of the Moon as it helps you against your enemies with the assistance of God's name IHOVA and ELOHIM, and angels Jahadiel and Azarel.

EVOCATION EXPERIENCES

TALERMAN

My first attempts to approach the part of the Moon where Emvatibe resides were not that successful. I remember that I was riding a bicycle up and down some high mountains and climbed some extremely long ladders, steps and stairs. At one moment, I saw Emvatibe's castle in the distance, and I even managed to get inside for a few seconds, but there I was just able to read two of his brief messages which he had apparently written to me. They were nailed on the wall. The one read: "More outdoor activities are required from you if you want to enter"; and the other: "Back to work."

In some of my later evocations, Emvatibe told me that there were many officers and soldiers in his regions, but that he was also responsible for some of the most peaceful, beautiful and tranquil landscapes of the Moon. At the end, he said, "Many exhausted human souls rest there," and then he vanished.

KADILIYA

It started with me walking along the beach shore until I saw something running towards me. The closer it got, the more it resembled an animal. Finally, it was a white horse with a crest on its chest. It came up to me and yanked my shirt with its teeth gently. The horse wanted me to take a ride, so I hopped on. We came to a place far off the cliff side of the beach. There was a castle. The horse dropped me off and disappeared into the mists. I was walking up the castle when I noticed a blue energy beam going through the castle gates. I did not see a door and there was nothing visible that would indicate that there was a way in. I looked around and saw a ladder glowing. The ladder was old and not steady, but that was my only way in, so I used it to climb over. Everything around me started to break down into tiny pixels until everything was gone. I was standing in nothingness. The tiny small pixels started forming something in front of me which eventually took a form of a man.

That man was wearing black a long trench coat and had long straight black hair. As soon as his arms and hands were visible, a sudden light reflected and I was blinded for a second, but my instincts kicked in and I dodged very suddenly. I was shocked and a little disorientated, so I looked around to see what was happening. I saw him standing not too far away from me holding a sword. He had a very determined look and came at me again. I don't know how that was possible, but I dodged many of his attacks and managed to grab his wrist. I pulled him towards me and took a step back. I didn't know what else to do, so I freaked out and he quickly pulled back and stood there staring at me. I somehow for sure knew I was being tested. He asked, "Where is your sword?" I replied, "Um, my sword? I'm not sure…" He was not happy with my answer because he had such a look in his eyes. He then said, "Well then, I shall put mine away". Then his sword disappeared, but he himself disappeared as well. Then he reappeared right in front of my face. I don't know how, but I seemed to have moved an inch just enough to dodge his hand that was about to attack me. I had zero time to think about anything. I was on high alert. He continued to attack me but I was managing to escape. As I decided not to run anymore, I turned back to him and waited for his next attack. For some reason, I could again dodge his attacks like last time. Now we started fighting hand-to-hand combat. At one point he grabbed my collar and I couldn't run away, but still managed to kick him in the head like a scorpion sting. I didn't know I could do that. He backed off and smiled. I suddenly felt the rush of energy of excitement as if I unlocked something very important. By this time I started attacking him. It was like dancing, to be honest. I didn't feel threatened or scared, and he wasn't being vicious either. He finally came to a full stop and said, "Come back to me when you've found your sword". He walked away slowly fading into the light and I found myself standing near the beach again.

Warning

The Picatrix's talisman: An armed man riding a cavalry horse holding a serpent in his right hand.
Agrippa's talisman: A soldier on a horse, holding a serpent in his right hand.
Bruno's image: A soldier sitting on a horse, holding a snake in his right hand and leading a black dog with his left.

Black magic can turn the **House of Protection against malevolent People** into the **House of Destruction.** According to Agrippa and some other medieval sources, Assurez wrath is useful for the destruction of cities, villages, buildings, fountains, wells, streams, and gold mines. It was also used for placing discord in general or between man and wife.

As Emvatibe is one of the mightiest warriors of the Moon, only the very advanced magician might have a chance to contact him. His talismans were traditionally made for black magic purposes. They were used to ignite enmity, separations, and the creation of evil desires.

Besides all these factors, some immature magicians might be tempted to use magical formulae obtained by Emvatibe just to satisfy their curiosity, which might be very dangerous as they have, according to Franz Bardon, the power to instantly kill people.

5th Genius – Amzhere

Arabian Name: Cabil
Western Tradition: Gabriel
Amzhere is the head of the 5th Mansion: Alchatay or Albachay
House of Favours: 21°25'40" Taurus - 4°17'09" Gemini
Picatrix's Talisman: The head of a man-made in silver. Above the head "Cabil" is written
Agrippa's Talisman: The head of a man
Bruno's Image: A prince on a silver throne, holding a rod in his right hand and embracing a girl with his left
Position of the 5th Mansion in the Moon Zone: Astral parts of the Moon

Amzhere looks like a kind, friendly and benevolent man. He usually wears a black coat with long sleeves, a white shirt and a black hat, but while he is performing liturgy, he is dressed in sacred white robes. When he is in a temple, he is in his angelic form. On less formal occasions, which is more often, he is like an ordinary person, but sometimes also looks like a wizard from a fairy tale. One of his names is Gabriel, so he must not be confused with Archangel Gabriel. They are two entirely different spirits. What connects them is the Moon, with which both of them are very closely related.

Amzhere teaches about: political sciences, social studies, law, art, writing, and child education. He is a very good guardian of newly married couples. This genius can also make you both physically powerful and mentally strong.

With Amzhere by your side, you will have all possible support from your friends, family and superiors. He can make you adored by important men and women alike. According to Franz Bardon, Amzhere can make the magician's "greatest enemy his friend at once" and "the heart of the hard men melt". Going back to the Picatrix, the Fifth Mansion is for receiving good things from kings and high officials. Some other genii from the Earth, Moon, Mercury and other planets can also help you with some very important people, but if you want to have good relations with Amzhere, he will be particularly interested in helping you with services from the highest possible levels of dignitaries since that is where his focus is on.

Amzhere, being a great guardian of families can help you find good schools and teachers for your children. He can help your children get good results in exams (in which he is similar to Porascho, a head from the Earth Zone). It is best to take your exams when the Moon is in the 5th Mansion, but if you maintain good relations with Amzhere, you are likely to become the best student in your group, regardless of the Moon's position in the sky. You may also get help from the school administration if you need it.

This genius is one of the best guardians of travellers, so he can also guard you are travelling abroad by aeroplane or boat. He is especially keen to protect the ones returning home from their travels. Ask this genius for help if you are at risk of missing the aeroplane or other means of transportation! Amzhere's pentacle will keep your journeys safe when the Moon is in other mansions too.

Amzhere rules over a region of the Moon which is silvery-dark, safe, silent, enjoyable, peaceful, static and tranquil. You may feel as if you were in a fairy tale when you reach his land.

In fact, his region is so beautiful that you might even start doubting its existence. Mysterious medieval castles are built thereupon unusually shaped mountaintops which are also interlinked with magnificently beautiful and ancient wooden hanging bridges. The nights are incredibly tranquil there. It is difficult to reach this paradise, but the same can be said about the inner areas of other mansions too. Quite typically, the first part of Alchatay has many obstacles, but most of the other mansions have hindrances as well. They have been set there to prevent people and other spirits from reaching the Lunar paradise before their time is up. The sky is not so magical and beautiful when you are far away from the Lunar paradise. It can even sometimes be grey and featureless. Many Amzhere's subordinate spirits are originally humans from our planet who became Lunar people after they had died. They do not need to reincarnate on Earth again anymore. They choose to continue to help from the Moon Zone rather than from the material part of the Earth, but some of them, who wish to be as close to living people as possible, do reincarnate voluntarily.

EVOCATION EXPERIENCES

TALERMAN

When I reached Amzhere's region, I felt exhausted, so I sat down on the ground to relax. I recovered my strength after a while, stood up, took a deep breath, and looked up at the sky. There I saw our blue planet.

Soon after, I was in a tavern where Amzhere was just holding a celebration together with all the other Lunar genii. He looked like a benevolent wizard. He had a black hat and a long black coat which looked as if it was from the early 19th Century. As he saw me, he stood up from his seat and approached me with a suit of cards in his hands. All other spirits stopped talking and drinking at that moment. They all looked at me curiously. Amzhere asked me to pick up a card from the suit, and I did what he said. It was a card with a picture of the angel Gabriel on it. Amzhere told me that the card I had chosen was his. Of all Lunar genii, I happened to choose him. Then he said that Gabriel is his traditional name, but that he is also known by other names too. When the two of us started talking, all the other spirits from the tavern cheered at us and then continued to celebrate.

I looked out the window. The night was black and silver, and also very peaceful. Something is always silver and peaceful in the blackness of the Moon's sky. I was thinking to myself that the most mystical nights can be nowhere else but on the Moon.

Another time, I saw Amzhere as a priest in a temple holding a ceremony together with two other angels. They were all dressed in white and sang beautifully. They looked as if they had just stepped out from medieval frescoes, except for the wings which they did not have. I heard them singing while the sky above the Moon was getting lighter. The Sun was rising. I realized that they were hailing the Sun. In the end, Amzhere told me enigmatically, "there are records of many things" in his region. Then he disappeared.

KADILIYA

I opened my eyes. I was in a blue lagoon surrounded by mountains and snow. I walked out but was not cold. I saw a man sitting on a bench with his arms spread out and one leg resting on another. I noticed the scenery he was looking at. It was the green field. I asked him if he was Amzhere even though I knew it was him. He turned to me, smiled and said, "You know that I am." I asked for his sigil and he drew it in the air. It was a circle with a dot at the centre. I instantly knew what his sigil stood for. He said, "So you understand the meaning behind this symbol?

Very good." I knew it in my heart, but could not really express it. The centre dot is you, your truth, and the circle is what revolves around you and what influences you to grow. But this is really simple put it this way.

He said, "Instincts, do you know what they mean? Or what they are?" I replied, "Well, they are about basic survival mode. Instincts to survive, to protect?" He said, "Well, yes, but that is just the simple layer. We are all made from something and that something is our core. As you can see, my core makes me who I am, and yours, well, being a human, your core is your instincts. All humans are made from that core. However, there is more to that. Some spirits are made from the essence of healing, which makes them great healers, so they have vast knowledge in the healing department."

As he continued, I noticed the slight vibration of peace coming from him. My troubling thoughts were creating self-doubt, but Amzhere helped me make a better relationship with my inner self, which made me think that he was a great diplomat. All my previous worries seemed so small and yet important enough to him to dissect them for me. He looked like a chilled-out - handsome - dude full of wisdom and foresight. He definitely read my mind, my heart and my soul.

WARNING

Black magic can turn the **House of Favors** into the **House of Broken Friendships**. According to the Picatrix, Cabil's wrathfulness can be used to destroy the friendship between two people.

By using negative Lunar energies from this Mansion, the magician may cause all kinds of problems among people and even turn friends into enemies. If controlled by this counter-genius, dignitaries and other very important people will refuse to offer you any help.

6ᵀᴴ Genius – Enchede

Arabian Name: Nedeyraphe
Western Tradition: Dirachiel
The Picatrix's Talisman: Two images from white wax facing each other and wrapped in white silk
Agrippa's Talisman: Two images embracing one another
Bruno's Image: Two men armed with discarded swords embrace each another
Enchede is the head of the 6ᵗʰ Mansion: Athanna or Alchaya (Small Star of Great Light)
House of Venus and Mars: 4°17'09" - 17° 08' 34" Gemini
Position of the 6ᵗʰ Mansion in the Moon Zone:
Enchede's residential part of the Moon is very large. One of its parts stretches out towards the Venus Zone, while the other borders the Mars Zone

Enchede has dualistic nature. This genius often appears either as a man to men or a woman to women. He is one of the best teachers of Martian and Venusian magic in the Moon Zone. This head is skilled at singing, writing and painting, but is also an expert in war history and warfare. Enchede has been depicted as a very gentle, adventurous and handsome man with grey hair looking like an older rock musician, but the other aspect of him is of a military or a police officer. He was seen dressed as a policeman in a blue uniform with shiny brass buttons down the front swinging a baton in his hand, but also as a singer welcoming people to the Moon with his beautiful voice. In her female form, Enchede was seen wearing clogs and a very long bright red coloured kimono with pink sakura blossom. Enchede told me once that, "her authority is granted by the stars". Some of Enchede's messages can be very personal and given under the seal of secrecy so that they cannot be published.

In Martian magic, if you happened to be an officer or soldier, Enchede might secure your victories over your enemies. According to Agrippa, the 6th Mansion conduces to hunting, besieging of towns, and revenge of princes. In the medieval "Ashmole 396 manuscript" it is written: "When the Moon is in this Mansion, kings may begin to war and to lay sieges and pursue enemies and malefactors." Additionally, Enchede provides high wages if you are in the military, but most importantly, he will make sure that the magician survives the war under any circumstances. Some of his lectures regarding warfare, such as its effects on creating belligerent and unpredictable egregores, are far advanced for our dimension. This genius can take you to the past so that you can also witness important battles and other military events with your own eyes. He also helps war prisoners, giving them freedom within a few days of their captivity. Thus, if someone you know happens to be in jail, ask for Enchade's help. No matter whether they are guilty or innocent, they will get released very quickly.

Enchede is a great hunter too. If you are a hunter, make sure to ask Enchede to be your guardian. Enchede closely cooperates with some of the most powerful beings from the woods, ancient hunter gods and descendants of Pan and Dionysus. He is a great friend of Petuno, a head from the Earth Zone whose faculty is hunting. Enchede can teach you how to become a great hunter/huntress out in the wild as well as for love or business opportunities.

Enchede is also a restless and eternal traveller in the sky. He brings safe journeys like many other genii from the Moon

Zone. He grants good time during the travel and coming on time. His other self manifests as the Naga in the night sky that either light the pathways for the adepts or actually becomes the black serpent that takes travellers to the Moon regions. In the ancient esoteric Tibetan texts, Naga comes in many forms, either as the stars of the night sky or the black river in the shape of a serpent that takes the adepts to the afterlife.

Related to the sphere of Venus, this genius teaches about sexual magic. According to Franz Bardon, Enchede instructs about "the charging of all kinds of talismans and amulets…with influences of the moon, by force of sexual magic". It has been also observed that the best time to start dating is when the Moon is in its 6th Mansion because then the powers of this angel are strongest. Enchede spreads friendship and love among people and makes strong and friendly alliances. If the magician is guarded or blessed by him, it will be a good time to start a new love adventure. Besides cabala, Enchede is an excellent teacher of tantra and sexual magic from all other mystical and magical traditions.

In esoteric mysticism, Enchede is one of the favourite spirits of Shaddai El Chai. (whom the Hermetic tradition presents as a mighty naked man as a symbol of his power in the creation of life). You may hear from Enchede many untold stories about Shaddai El Chai and his partner Shekina, a divine female aspect of Malkuth. He may encourage magically trained human couples to focus on the union of Shaddai El Chai and Shekina during their sexual intercourse. According to Enchede, life on Earth is created from the union of Shaddai El Chai and Shekina who remind us that sex is a Divine act which creates life.

Additional Observations Relevant to Enchede's Teachings

Shaddai El Chai and Shekina

Gershom Scholem, a Jewish cabalist, has said, that the name of this Divine couple is El-Chai-Shekinah. According to Raphael Pata, a Hungarian historian, some Jewish couples were experiencing an orgasm while they were out of their bodies during their sexual encounters on Fridays after midnight. Abraham Abele Halevi Gombiner, a Polish rabbi from the 17th century, observed that some great cabalists used to write some of their biggest mysteries just after midnight inspired by their sexual practices.

Warfare

In wartime, the magician should be also additionally protected by the pentacles of Mars.

Evocation Experiences

Talerman

Something sinister was hiding behind the Moon's yellowish mist. If I showed any sign of fear, I knew that I would be instantly drawn back to the Earth, so I managed to calm down waiting for the mist to lift. As the scene was clearing up, I suddenly found myself sitting in the audience in front of a stage where a band was about to have a performance. Enchede entered the stage, looked directly at me and told me with a friendly voice, "Don't worry. I am not a malevolent spirit. Why are you afraid of me?" A very beautiful female singer stood by his side.

She told me that the two of them were about to sing a song about Luna to me. As they told me to relax and enjoy, in the next few minutes I was hearing them singing so beautifully with their angelic voices. The song is difficult for me to describe because it was not from our world.

A few years later, I saw Enchede again. He was again on the stage, but this time he was singing with two male members, a guitarist player and a drummer. When he saw me, he interrupted the song they were playing to introduce me to the whole audience. He told them that I am his friend and a guest from Earth.

The third time I saw him, it was something different because he was showing me the Mars magic. I went back in time with him to witness some of the most dramatic battles from WWI during the occupation of my country. While we were watching the horrendous scenes of war destruction, he spoke about the disastrous effects of modern warfare upon nature, the atmosphere and human health. He told me, "Bomb explosions create new artificial salamanders, sylphs and other elementals, which would otherwise never appear naturally. That is the reason why they are so unpredictable and why they often leave harmful consequences behind."

KADILIYA

I started seeing black and white countdown, 3, 2, 1. Then I found myself at a big theatre looking at a stage with a screen. The screen was turned on and it was black and white. I saw a tall person walking towards my direction and approaching the screen. Then I saw the feet coming out of the screen. This person was wearing clogs and a very long bright red coloured dress. Around the waist, there was the kimono-style belt. The chest was curved. Around the centre of her throat, there was a golden flower pattern which looked like a four-pointed star. The back of the kimono was a very long drape hanging down. Then I saw this person's lips which were coloured bright red. I realized this was a woman. She had big eyes with eyeliner and straight-cut fringe. The rest of the hair was tied back.

She came close to me and said, "I am Enchede, nice to meet you. I have come to your calls". I was so surprised because I didn't expect this spirit to take a female form. Then she took my hand and asked me to go with her and I did. We walked into the screen and we came to a village. There were lots of small pyramids around. Some people were looking at us curiously. Then we came to a pond which was pink coloured. We stood in the centre of the pond and she waved around when the water came over us like a giant sphere which closed us in. From here on the journey with her took a turn. She told me that I wasn't ready and to evoke her again when I am. After that everything collapsed and I returned.

Warning

Black magic can turn the **Mansion of Venus and Mars** into the **Mansion of Violence and Destruction.** According to the Picatrix, Nedeyrahe wrathful presides over the destruction and the besieging of cities with armies. He destroys crops and trees and makes medicines ineffective. Due to such influences, in wartime, sexual energies may get distorted turning people to lust for revenge, rape, killing and violence. Even mature magicians should be careful after evoking Enchede, in order not to raise within themselves uncontrollable sexual lust and some bizarre sexual desires.

Some cabalists say that Gamaliel, the commander of the demonic order of the Ogiels and the queen of the night Lilith stands for unhealthy and generated relations between the Moon and the Earth as an opposite side to the divine relations between

Shaddai El Chai and Shekina. Eliphas Levi has claimed that Gamaliel is a fallen cherub and that he is subordinated to Lilith. Yet, many magicians do not agree with such comparisons since they honour Lilith as a goddess of the Moon and reject insinuations of her as an evil spirit. Ask Enchede for advice if you happened to be interested to learn more about relations between Gamaliel and Lilith in a safe manner!

7th Genius – Emrudue

Arabian Name: Selehe or Siely
Western Tradition: Schliel
The Picatrix's Talisman: Two images from white wax, facing each other, and wrapped in white silk
Agrippa's Talisman: A man well clothed, holding his hands up to heaven in praying and supplicating
Bruno's Image: A well-dressed man in a silver chair, holding both hands up towards the skies in supplication
Emrudue is the head of the 7th Mansion: Aldimiach or Alazarach (Hand of Gemini)
House of All Good Things: 17°08'34" Gemini - 0°0'0" Cancer
Position of the 7th Mansion in the Moon Zone: Emrudue's region is a paradise-like part of the Moon. People who live there enjoy their endless days in one of the most beautiful astral regions of our planetary system

Emrudue is one of the most benevolent spirits from the Moon Zone. He often appears as a muscular black man. He is very similar to the third genius Ezhesekis, as both of them like to be active in the physical world and secure success in all earthly matters. Emrudue's mission is to fulfil all your wishes especially in bringing forth abundance and prosperity in various means.

The 7th Mansion of the Moon has much in common with Nine of Cups in tarot. It is a "wishing card" of all the Moon mansions. Traditionally, the 7th Mansion gives good luck and success in all fields and in all earthly matters. It marks a good time for partnership, lovers, making peace, strengthening friendships and travelling (though delays are possible on return trips). According to the Picatrix, it is also good for trade, profit, safe travel, crops, the friendship between friends and allies and benefits in the presence of kings and high nobles. He is also one of the strongest protectors of travellers. Ask this genius for help if you want to have a safe and comfortable travel. This genius also helps politicians if their goals are noble. If you are a scholar, Emrudue will find you a way to teach at the best possible schools or become a very popular teacher with great knowledge and authority.

Franz Bardon agrees with the traditional views about this genius and adds, "If a person not initiated into magic wears the seal of the seventh head of the Moon sphere, manufactured during the astrological period of the seventh moon station and engraved on a silver plate, he or she will have good luck and success and above all, have any earthly desire fulfilled." According to the modern astrologer Christopher Warnock, this Mansion signifies success, particularly in business and trade. It is the Mansion of abundance and wealth. All in all, it is always good to make a wish when the Moon is in the 7th Mansion, especially when it is waxing. Emrudue may definitely help you find your lucky star. If you want to make it sure that he hears your wishes, write a petition on a piece of paper and put it on your triangle next to Emrudue's sigil, during the evocation. You can also keep that paper on your altar afterwards.

Evocation Experiences

Talerman

Emrudue asked me what I wished for and when I told him, he said he would support me. He also showed me a very simple method of making a wish come true: As you are making a wish, mix a bowl of water with a magic wand!

Not all visions from Emrudue have been beautiful, though. Once, he guided me through nightmares in which I heard him saying: "Wounded people lose their legs and arms and are distraught in pain". His remarks were followed by horrific scenes of bloody battles which made me pray for world peace and love among all people. Emrudue told me that when advanced magicians have nightmares or horrible visions of future catastrophic events, they have the power to prevent them through their prayers.

Kadiliya

I came to a circular door. It was narrow, so I had to crawl through until I came to a room which was large and square. Everything was lit up. I looked around and I saw a man crossed legged sitting in the centre of the room. He was muscular, black, and wearing a white scarf around his head and face. His eyes were shut. It looked like he was meditating. I did not want to bother him so I sat somewhat in front of him and went into my own meditation. However, I could not leave that room. Everything I could see and sense was within that room. I saw a barrier between me and this spirit. It was like an energy veil that was golden between us. I did not speak but only observed my surroundings since I could not do much. Then I heard his voice, that vibration was an instant tell that this was Emrudue.

He walked up to me in my meditation and put a square energy thing all around me and drew a symbol on the top. He then with his deep voice said, "Observe your energy level". I saw my energy collapsing from the top all the way down. I felt fine though. In fact, I felt more recharged. He said, "You must ground yourself while working, this is a gift for you. You may use this method whenever you feel you must ground yourself. Make it a habit. This has taken a lot from you and you must realize it is important to ground yourself." I noticed an instant change in my energy level and felt warmer and connected to the ground. I asked for his sigil and he drew it in the air, then he said, "This is all I will offer, for now, strengthen your base". Then I left with this square energy box thing hanging around me. It seems like it will be there all day, but I was shown how to create it at will so I will give it a go again soon.

Warning

Black magic **House of All Good Things** into **House of Regret** influences such circumstances in which people would later regret that their wishes have come true. According to the Picatrix, Siely wrathful presides over the destruction of officials.

Emrudue's ideal is happiness to all people thus he will not fulfil your wish if it is to bring any form of harm to others. The most challenging part of this Mansion is in the saying: 'Be careful what you wish for, it might just come true!' It is a variation of an old Yiddish curse. It is also a theme in stories about the Devil who grants your wish, but not exactly the way you want it, because of your failure to specify all the details and the conditions. It is usually about people who say that they wish for something before thinking if they really want it.

8ᵀᴴ Genius – Eneye

Arabian Name: Annediex
Western Tradition: Amnediel
Picatrix's Talisman: An image of an eagle with the head of a man. In its breast, it is inscribed the name of the lord of this Mansion
Agrippa's Talisman: An eagle having the face of a man
Bruno's Image: A man riding an eagle, with a palm in his right hand, followed by two captives
Eneye is the head of the 8th Mansion: Alnaza or Anatrachya (Cancer)
House of Victory: 0°0'0"-12°51'22" Cancer
Position of the 8ᵗʰ Mansion in the Moon Zone: Not specified. Different parts of this Mansion can be found all over the Moon Zone

Eneye is often seen as a very tall male spirit with dark hair. He is one of the most powerful heads of the Moon. His faculties are connected to military, political and diplomatic events, so he may help the magician become a successful military officer, politician or diplomat.

According to the Picatrix, the 8th Mansion helps to achieve victory. Magicians from the past took the talisman of Annediex into battle to be victorious and prevail over everyone. If you are an officer or soldier, ask this angel to be your guardian. When Eneye is evoked by a magician who has the potential in politics, he will encourage him or her, simply because he thinks that nowadays our world would benefit from mature magicians involved in politics. Furthermore, if the magician is a significant public figure, he or she can petition for Eneye's protection. Eneye is one of the leaders of the diplomatic corps from the Moon Zone and all of the Lunar foreign missions in our Solar system are under his control. He also closely cooperates with Paschy, a leader of all the diplomats from the Earth Zone.

Eneye teaches the magician how to use the Moon magic not only to be victorious in the fields of military and politics but in any other profession or any other aspects of life too. He can make the magician well respected by peers, in business, school and career in general. If you are in a debate team or trying to win over some important people, ask for Eneye's help. Magicians who are CEOs and have some special political ties will also benefit from having Eneye's protection and help. Be mindful that it should be a profession to your liking, though!

This genius is also one of the best guardians of travellers. His speciality is to provide the magician with the excellent company during trips. If you are a lone traveller, he will accompany you with some very interesting passengers sitting next to you when you travel. He will make your journeys safe and fast. If you are late, remember to ask this angel for help!

On an interesting note, old grimoires mention that this angel helps "chase away mice and flies", which in modern terminology would mean the elimination of epidemics through hygiene and sanitation.

The last but not least, when it comes to bad weather conditions, Eneye is capable of changing it in your favour while bringing joy.

Additional Observations Relevant to Eneye's Teachings on Protection

In wartime, you may also additionally need Mars' pentacles for protection.

Evocation Experiences

Talerman

Eneye introduced me to a group of his subordinate spirits. All of them were gracious and elegantly dressed. I asked one of them, a very beautiful female spirit if she could tell me an unknown secret about the 28 Mansions of the Moon, which I could later publish. So, she told me that the Moon Zone does not only consist of 28 Mansions but that it has millions of different regions too. She noticed that I was very surprised, so she told me that the Moon Zone is much larger than people could ever imagine. She also told me that she had been a Muslim during her life on Earth. She need not tell me that, but I knew that she was an angel.

Kadiliya

I was seeing far into space and time. Everything felt like it was zooming into something until I saw a clear view of a giant green forest. The middle of the forest was completely white. I landed there and noticed it was covered with ice. At the centre, there were flowers and also a man wearing blue clothes.

He had dark hair and was very tall and broad. He was watering the flowers. I went up to him and asked if he was Eneye and he confirmed. I asked about his sigil and he drew it in the air.

He asked me, "What can I do for you?", and I explained my position. He thought about it for a moment and said, "Hm, Isis...that is a nice name. I see what you lack currently. Would you like me to show you?", and I said yes. He pointed his hand down and slowly moved it, then the ground formed a thin layer of ice. He looked at me and said, "Walk on this". I stepped onto the ice and started walking, but treading very carefully scared of falling down. Then I made my way back. He said, "Did you notice how you walked?", and I said I did. He continued, "Each step you took, you were very careful and anxious. You did not put much weight and you weren't comfortable. Contemplate on that. I do not have any more to teach nor show you". Then I left.

Warning

Black magic can transform the **House of Victory** into the **House of Merciless.** According to the Picatrix, Annediex wrathful presides over making the incarceration of captives firm and the destruction and affliction of captives.

Eneye is a friendly spirit, peacemaker and diplomat, and he likes noble people. His influence will lead you to victory, but when you win, he will also respect you if you would show mercy to the side you defeated. When winners show no mercy to the defeated opponents, not only in war, but also in sports, competitions, debates, business ventures, and all other aspects of life, you may ask Eneye to intervene.

9ᵀᴴ Genius – Emzhebyp

Arabian Name: Raubel
Western Tradition: Barbiel
Emzhebyp is the head of the 9ᵗʰ Mansion: Archaam or Arcaph
House of Health: 12°51'22"- 25°42'51" Cancer
Position of the 9ᵗʰ Mansion in the Moon Zone: Not specified, but looks paradise-like
Talismans and Images: Traditionally used for malevolent purposes, so they are presented in the 'Warning' section of this entry.

Emzhebyp is often portrayed as a male spirit with vast knowledge in the mental health department correlating to the lunar cycles. He often appears in either a long white or red garment. Features of his face may seem to be disproportionately large and exaggerated. He can help you heal: epilepsy, gynaecological diseases, hysteria, obsessions and St. Vitus' dance. This genius can teach you how to prevent all Lunar-related diseases caused by the negative effects of the Moon. No matter what modern medicine says about lunacy, Emzhebyp will encourage the magician to treat it as a special mental disorder caused by the Moon and treat their patients accordingly. Emzhebyp is certainly one of the best healers from the Moon Zone.

Science has not proven any connections between Lunar rhythms and menstrual cycles, because it mostly anticipates that the similarity in length between the two cycles is likely coincidental. Nonetheless, magicians who have fertility issues, want to heal or are purely curious about this subject, may ask Emzhebyp to teach them about the Moon's relation with fertility and how it corresponds to the female menstrual cycle which averages 28 days to fully understand this system.

Emzhebyp is one of the few genii from the Moon who is not meant to be a guardian of travellers. When the Moon is in its 9th Mansion, Emzhebyp suggests we be passive, stay at home and avoid travelling. This Mansion signifies that it is a good time for meditation, relaxation and studies.

Additional observations relevant to Emzhebyp's teachings

Lunatics

Old Romans back in the day recognized that the cycles of the Moon could periodically influence some sensitive people in a negative way. They called those people "lunatics". Until the 18th Century, medical and judicial documents distinguished lunatics from other psychic disorders. In the 19th Century some people with periodical psychic crises, otherwise normal for the rest of the year, were recorded as "the lunatics", but they are no longer acknowledged as a special group of people in need. They are erased from modern medical and legal contexts and excluded from all medical research under that name. In fact, they are put in the same category as all other mental diseases. In 2012 the US House of Representatives passed legislation removing the word "lunatic" from all the federal laws in the USA. Lunatic diseases are no longer officially recognized in many parts of the world, so they cannot be formally treated either.

Lunar-Related Diseases

In order to prevent epilepsy and periodical attacks of madness, the magician may additionally evoke the lunar genius Pi-Job, whose name is written on the 6th Pentacle of the Moon. Alongside Emzhebyp, the Olympic spirit Phul is also good at healing diseases affected by the Moon. Antaura, a Greek female demon of migraine, was said to go out of the sea, move like the wind, and roar like a deer, before entering into a person's body which she would then cause terrible suffering. She is also the commander of many other demons of headaches but can be stopped by evoking the goddess Artemis.

Evocation Experiences

Talerman

Emzhebyp appeared yesterday as soon as I evoked him. His presence was very strong, doors opened and closed throughout the ritual. He said that he would like to teach me his magic.

My ritual lasted for some two hours. I transformed into a bird flying high up in the sky from where I could see large regions of the Earth and the Moon below me. While I was flying I was thinking that I was in a fairy tale. The scenery was so extraordinarily divine in its beauty that made me think that such things were so fantastic that they could not possibly be true. It made me cry and I thanked God for the beauty of his creation.

The last time I evoked Emzhebyp, he gave me to read a mystical script written in some unknown letters and then guided me to the Moon where he gave me an amethyst for a present in order to use it for healing.

KADILIYA

I sent off a vibration of his name and I came across this spirit in the bright space. He manifested himself as having long straight hair with white strands parted from his left. He was wearing a long white garment. He told me to be aware of the people around me. He said, "Contemplate and learn!". He also suggested I advocate my time of the day better because my mental energy is spent. Then he gave me a book, and when I took it, it kind of went inside me. I told him I couldn't read the book because it vanished and he told me, "All in good time when You need them, the tools will come out." Then he hugged me and left.

WARNING

The Picatrix's talisman: Image of a man with no genitalia, with his hands covering his eyes. Upon his neck, the name of the lord of this Mansion is written.
Agrippa's talisman: The image of a man wanting his privy parts, shutting his eyes with his hands.
Bruno's image: A eunuch with his hands over his eyes, in front of a dirty bed.

Black magic can turn **The House of Health** into the **House of Diseases.** According to the Picatrix, the 9th Mansion is for creating weakness and infirmity.
Some magicians from the past used those talismans to make people fall ill. Some immature people may also today be tempted to contact evil spirits in order to encourage epidemics and suffering.

10th Genius – Emnymar

Arabian Name: Aredafir
Western Tradition: Ardifiel
Picatrix's Talisman: Image from the gold of the head of a lion, above which the name of the lord of this Mansion is written
Agrippa's Talisman: The head of a lion
Bruno's Image: A woman giving birth, and in front of her a golden lion and a man appearing as a convalescent
Emnymar is the head of the 10th Mansion: Algelioche, Albegha, or Albegh (Throat of Leo)
House of Children: 25°42'51" Cancer - 8°34'17" - Leo
Position of the 9th Mansion in the Moon Zone: Close to the fairies' realm

Emnymar is a very benevolent spirit and a great friend of humankind. He is one of the best protectors of children and pregnant women. This genius has close relations with the archangels Sandalphon and Gabriel. During your evocations of Emnymar, you might see one of those two archangels by your side too.

Emnymar's help is often related to secrets of procreation and pregnancy. His primary mission is to protect women when they deliver babies. In the Picatrix, it is said that the 10th Mansion is for the "healing of illness and ease of childbirth in women."

Franz Bardon wrote,

....all gynecologists, midwives and their assistants are under his influence.

Emnymar closely cooperates with Arioth (19° Libra), a head from the Earth Zone who also protects women when they deliver babies and decides about a child's gender. In order to prevent painful deliveries and other problems during pregnancy, call Emnymar for help! The magician who evokes Emnymar, not only has a successful delivery but can also bring a pregnant woman to a good gynecologist.

Relations between mothers and their very young children are guarded by this spirit. We can ask this genius to be our guardian if we are teachers, educators, or parents, or if we share the same space or are connected with children in any other way too. Emnymar encourages the magician to take care of children and powerless people, promote love and charity, and increase love and devotion. He is also a guardian of love and friendship.

Emnymar also closely cooperates with Dosom (11° Taurus), a head from the Earth Zone, in teaching the magician about the secrets of mesmerism (animal magnetism), hypnotism, magnetic healing and parapsychology. Emnymar is also known to treat venereal diseases. He helps women reconnect to their own wombs. According to his teaching, endometriosis are clots of despair and rejection of one's own feminine body. Emnymar helps one to understand the true meaning of miscarriages and brings darkness from the death of a newborn to the light.

Emnymar is a special protector of widows and divorced women. Anyone who falls under those two categories can ask Emnymar for help to find new partners or to cope with being a widow.

This genius is very closely connected to witches. He can teach them to: be successful in love, bless friends, communicate with spirits, search for lost treasures, understand the voices of the winds, transform water into wine, divine with cards, read from palms, heal, transform ugliness into beauty, and tame wild beasts.

Emnymar is the king of many Lunar fairies, so he is one of the best spirits to ask for help if you want to get closer to the fairies' realm. He can help you connect with Diana's daughters who are fairies.

Additional Observations Relevant to Emnymar's Teachings on Diana's Daughters

One night, a poor young man with a good heart, saw thousands of small fairies flickering in white colours under the Full Moon. He was astonished by their beauty: "Oh, fairies, I would like so much to be like you! I would like to be carefree and without a need to eat. Who are you?" One fairy replied, "We are the Moonlights, Diana's daughters. We are daughters of the Moon. We were born from the light. When the Moon throws its lights, they appear in the shapes of fairies. And you are also one of us because you were born when the Moon, our mother Diana, was Full...And when you are hungry, poor and without money, just think about your mother Diana and tell: - My Luna, my Luna. More beautiful than any star! You are eternally beautiful! If you may reward me with good luck!" In the end, the fairies explained to the young man that children born during the Full Moon on Sunday are the sons and daughters of the Moon.

Evocation Experiences

Talerman

My evocations of this genius are usually fairy-like. Most probably due to this angel's influences, during my evocations of this spirit, my children often dream that they are on the Moon.

After one such dream, my son told me that he had never dreamed of anything so beautiful before in his life. My astral projections had guided me several times to the past to see my mother and other relatives from my previous lives, but later I learned that those experiences were most often actually supervised by Emnymar.

Kadiliya

I entered a space between here and there. That space was not so much astral. Perhaps it was more mental. Right at the beginning, I saw Archangel Gabriel standing next to me. I asked for his aid and he agreed and kind of vanished.

I called upon and vibrated Aredafir from the house of Alebha, but it lead me nowhere. So I started vibrating "Emnymar" from Bardon's book and suddenly something started pulling me deeper into space. I did not resist because it actually felt exciting.

I don't know where I was, but I saw little white flowers blossoming near my feet. I also saw a river stream running in front of me. The air tasted sweet and so did the water. I walked into the water and it almost felt like soft silk. I kept walking and I went deeper. I heard a voice telling me to lie down. I did it facing up and felt the water running through my hair softly like a brush. Then the voice said, "Let go, let go of the preconceived notions of this place, let it all go". Then I saw all my mental anxieties (such as what was this place again? What did he represent?) just flow away. Then I got up and started walking out, but I felt something underneath me pushing me up, and soon enough, I was riding a giant water horse. It was running so elegantly and it was powerful. I felt powerful and fearless. I felt the air on my face; it was sweet and fresh. The voice came back again and told me to let go of all the hesitations and let myself out. At that point, I felt exhilarated and full of joy marching forth like a warrior. Then I looked above and I saw myself riding a horse; the same scenario except upside down. Suddenly, the horse I was riding stopped at the edge of a cliff. I stepped down and decided to cross. To my surprise, I stepped on what seemed like thin ice. I kept walking looking below and I saw myself doing the same underneath me, like a mirror image. It was fun. I noticed each step I took on that ice the colour changed to red. My every step made a red-coloured ripple effect. The red was more like blood. I decided to go in, so I dived in. I was swimming in this red sea. There was a moment of stillness, but I was not afraid. In the water, I saw certain images like different scenes of a movie inside air bubbles. I went closer and got pulled in.

I was in my mother's arms as a baby. Then everything shuffled and I was walking on my own umbilical cord all the way up to the spirit realm. I saw myself watching my mother. But I felt different as if I was huge and I knew everything. I was watching my mother on earth, witnessing her compassion towards all humanity and her true willpower. Her sternness, willpower and compassion were what I needed to come through and incarnate on earth. I needed a strong person who could carry me and my consciousness through this world. It was her pure heart of compassion and strong willpower that gave birth to me. I felt so much joy and love. At that point, I had a sudden understanding: a mother's mental and emotional conditions during her nine months of pregnancy will strongly impact her child's emotional and mental growth in the future. This is a karmic tie. A child can grow up living in their mother's shadow for a long time without realizing it. However, this itself is also a huge catalyst for that child's spiritual growth. Once realized and understood, that veil can be lifted so the growth of that child can finally begin. It is like leading the path to self-awakening. From here on there were personal messages from Emnymar that are most relevant to me.

I came out from all that feeling like a warrior both mentally and emotionally. I saw Emnymar standing before me. I thanked him for everything he had shown me and he replied, "It is my honour and my pleasure." I asked him what he is associated with and he replied, "New birth, literally and metaphorically. I show the relationship between the spirit and the physical." I also saw him helping people who came to him with whatever was needed for them. However, to truly work with him, you must let go of everything. Let him take you on a journey and see where that leads!

Warning

According to some old scripts, this Mansion is not good for borrowing money and travelling. Otherwise, if you are a mature magician and work with Emnymar with respect, magic with this spirit can hardly have any counter-effects. One branch of this spirit's faculties is related to mesmerism, which powers, according to Franz Bardon,

> ......*must never be used for dishonourable intentions, because counter-effects and counter-genii are likely to occur if you do otherwise.*

Emnymar will refuse to work with anyone that asks to do their malevolent bidding. Anyone who forces this spirit to such tasks will bring misfortune in areas of marriage, childbirth, and relationships with family to themselves.

Have in mind that this spirit is always very closely associated with the Laws of Karma.

11ᵀᴴ Genius – Ebvep

Arabian Name: Necol
Western Tradition: Neciel
Picatrix's Talisman: A man riding a lion, holding a lance in his right hand and holding the ear of the lion with his left hand. The name of the lord of this Mansion is written in front of this figure
Agrippa's Talisman: A man riding a lion, holding the ear thereof in his left hand, and in his right, holding forth a bracelet of gold
Bruno's Image: A man riding a lion, holding its mane in his left hand and a small lance in his right
Ebvep is the head of the 11th Mansion: Azobra or Ardaf (Leo's Crest)
House of Respect: 8°34'17" - 21°25'40" Leo
Position of the 11th Mansion in the Moon Zone: Close to the Sun Zone

Ebvep is a very powerful, tall and beautiful female genius. Her first appearance may give an impression of a black lady surrounded by red, silver or green sparks of light. She is not easily seen during evocations, but the trained magician may feel her strong presence. Franz Bardon has warned that it is difficult to evoke Ebvep, for which reason he suggested the guidance of some other relevant heads of the Earth Zone instead.

Ebvap teaches about manifestations on all levels. She is known as the grand master of the phenomenal magic of the Moon Zone. She can create some of the most fantastic magical phenomena, which would make, as Franz Bardon has remarked, "a non-initiate tremble with dread and horror". If you are a stage artist, this spirit may help you impress the audience with many magical tricks and phenomena. In this respect, Ebvep closely cooperates with the following masters of phenomenal magical of the Earth Zone: Nimtrix (15° Cancer), Camalo (14° Cancer), Camalo (24° Taurus), Pagalusta (26° Leo), and Agasoly (27° Sagittarius).

As a master of manifestation, she gives instructions about how to materialize things from the astral plane into our world. She can give you inspiration and confidence to push an idea (that is still in the astral plane) towards its materialization in the physical realm. If you want to improve your manifesting abilities from the astral to the material or otherwise, seek Ebvep's help, and not only will your abilities improve, but your life can significantly change for the better too.

Another aspect of Ebvap's abilities is that she is able to ensure very high respect for magicians regardless of their social status or rank. Alongside a few other genii from the Earth and the Moon Zone, Ebvep helps the magician receive timely help from very important people. This spirit grants: power, profit, wealth, gain, and promotions.

You may also ask this spirit to give freedom to prisoners. The last but not least, call Ebvep to be your guardian while travelling on land!

Ebvap has many things in common with the main spirit of the tarot card Strength.

She is also one of the guardians of the number 9. In magic, this numerical value is connected to the Moon. The number 9 crystallizes elemental energies and it stands for the last phase of the Lunar manifestations before they would materialize as solid matters in the number 10. Ebvep may tell the magician many other secrets about the number 9 which has not been revealed to anyone before. You may also ask Ebvep to help you create the most powerful engrams. In most of their forms, the engrams enhances manifestations on the Earth in positive or negative forms; and it is up to the magician what to choose. Some shapes of the engrams contain positive and negative powers and in such combinations, they may harm alchemical principles.

Additional Observations Relevant to Ebvap's Teaching

Number 9

Franz Bardon confirms that everything which comes from the Lunar sphere has influence in 9. Pseudo-Dionysius the Areopagite has said that there are 9 orders of angels. There are also 9 heavenly realms. Some Buddhists believe that heaven has 9 fields and 9999 angles. Zeus created 9 muses in his 9 love affairs and Chinese cinnabar becomes drinkable after 9 transformations. 9 is the last number; it announces the end and the new start and it also contains an idea of death and rebirth, especially materially, one's self, strengths and weaknesses of an individual, insights and wisdom.

Enegrams

Engrams represent Yesod and they help the magician's connections to the Moon. The most beneficial, potent and benevolent engram is "The Star of Luna" or "Kether's engram" because it represents the energetic stamp of all existing virtues of our Solar system and contains the highest aspects of Luna.

Materialization

If the Moon keeps its door closed for you, your chances to make a manifestation of any kind will be small. Your ideas will remain in the sphere of the astral world with little chance to be materialized in our world's reality. The First Pentacle of the Moon serves for opening up the Moon's door in all situations. If you get stuck in your life, this pentacle can help you find a way out, but also, quite literally, it can save you if you are trapped in your car, lift or prison. The names of the following angels are written on the left side of the pentacle: Yashiel, Shioel, Vaol and Vehiela. The God's names written on the right side are IHV, IHOVA, AL and AHH; and in the middle: IHOVA. There is also a verse from Psalm 107:16, which can be used for the same purpose in conjurations.

Evocation Experiences

Talerman

It was more convenient for me to evoke Ebvep in her traditional name (Necol or Neciel), but other magicians might find it easier to evoke her by her name Ebvep. You should evoke this and other spirits using both of their alternate names until you find out what works better for you in any given situation.

I spent half of the night with this angel, half of the time in my room and the other half in her own lunar realms. She talked a lot about the number 9 and the secrets of materialization. She told me that I could count on her help if I needed to get in touch with some very important people.

𝒦ADILIYA

I was having an intense headache so it was a little difficult to focus. I started seeing Ebvep's name floating around and the letters were being swapped around. Then they changed into coloured letters. They were dancing around and looked like auroras. I went up the sky to reach them and they formed into steps. I started walking up the steps when I noticed that I was bare feet and holding a bow and arrows. I threw the arrows away and they fell like meteor showers. I came through a door and when I turned back, the door vanished and I was in complete brightness. It was snowing. My head was hurting too much so I laid down. I was watching the snow falling and slowly landing on my face. The sky was clear, though. I saw some clouds that were forming the name Ebvep. The clouds vibrated and vanished. Another cloud came by and did the same. I lay there for a while. I did not want to get up. There was a sense of peace but also sadness that came over my body.

I heard Ebvap's voice loud and clear which lead to us conversing for a while. These were some of the things she said: "Your human society is built upon chaos. It thrives on chaos. However, there is also order. People like you work on bringing order, so in the end, it balances things out. One cannot live without light and dark, chaos and order, negative and positive. Your density is all about the two sides of the coin."

I asked, "How do you walk away from the chaos before you lose yourself in it?" And she said, "Take a moment of a deep breath. Within that single moment of drawing in the breath, let your mind wonder! Will chaos show the truth? Your truth? What are you trying to achieve? You will have moments of utter frustration. You will dance with fire, but you will be also burned and brought to exhaustion and pain. That is merely one vibration not being able to harmonize with the other. If you have that level of awareness, then you will become the tuner of frequencies". I asked her, "What is your prime role?" She replied,

"Relationships between mankind and spirits. I am that voice you hear when you need a reason and an understanding, especially during situations where you need a mediator. I am that counsel of support."

Another thing we discussed was the truth of our hearts. When we get pulled into someone's chaos, we often forget about our own hearts. Our society is pretty much reactionary. We do not very much nurture the heart and therefore the truth is not spoken very much. People forget, so they react by defending their egos, beliefs, and agendas, even if it makes no sense. We discussed how to recognize these things in ourselves and in others, and also how to combat them. I thanked her for her help.

Warning

Black magic can turn the **House of Respect** into the **House of Arrogance.**

You might become a very powerful person but also arrogant and cruel as a side-effect of working with Ebvep. This is such a powerful spirit, that you may also expect headaches and exhaustion during the evocation and also afterwards.

12th Genius – Emkepbe

Arabian Name: Abdizu
Western Tradition: Abdizuel
Emkepbe is the head of the 12th Mansion: Alzarpha, Azarfa, or Azarpha (Leo's Tail)
House of Peace and Love: 21°25'40" Leo - 4°17'09" Virgo
Position of the 12th Mansion in the Moon Zone: There are a lot of waters in Emkepbe's region. This is mostly a watery part of the Moon
Talismans and Images: Presented in the 'Warning' section because they were traditionally used for malevolent purposes

Emkepbe is an angel of peace and love. He has a long face, long nose, and hooded eyes with small eyebrows. This genius has long hair tied back like in a Mongolian. He looks very Asian or maybe even more like a Native American. Emkepbe often appears as a fatherly figure to some magicians.

His services about love matters are very similar to Enchede, the 6th genius of the Moon. The difference is mostly in that Emkepbe is more specifically up to help couples who are married or about to get married, while Enchede helps everybody. Emkepbe is certainly one of the greatest guardians of marriages.

This angel helps singles find new romantic partners and he can also teach the magician how to make amulets to bring: love, sympathy, peace and friendship. Emkepbe's influence can help newlyweds or couples to stay happy together by encouraging lots of fun activities which they can enjoy together such as hiking, dining, partying, shopping, travelling and meeting friends. If couples seek higher self-development and awareness, Emkepbe can help them enrich their spiritual lives as well. When working alongside Emkepbe, there is a tendency of attracting a lot of friends.

Magicians whose occupation is in the field of long-term traveling (such as sailing), can benefit from asking Emkepbe to be their protector. They can ask him to bring stability in love and marriages when far away. He helps people when they travel, especially on water.

All in all, Emkepbe is one of the best teachers of water magic in the Moon Zone.

Additional Observations Relevant to Emkepbe's Teachings on Protection

The Third Pentacle of the Moon protects from all dangers from the water and it should be carried while you travel. The hand on the pentacle is directed towards the names of the angels Aub and Vevafel. There is also a verse in the pentacle from Psalm 40:13, which is useful in a case of danger.

EVOCATION EXPERIENCES

TALERMAN

Emkebpe appeared in my room and I started my mental communication with him. He confirmed to me that his main faculty is to bring peace into one's life. Emkebpe also said that among all of the marriages in the world, those which have special protection from the Moon, are the happiest. Before he went away, he told me to call him if I am anxious, and he promised to bring peace to my heart and mind.

KADILIYA

I started to trace his name in my mental mind using energy and slowly vibrating it, but I already felt his presence way before. I saw his face so clearly. He turned to his left side to look at me. He was gold and white. I was at an empty dark space, but in front of me, I saw a white flame. I instantly got excited. I came close to the flames and I walked in. My skin, or a layer of me that was black, started to disappear. I saw myself but I was more like an energy. I felt like I grew bigger and taller. Then I saw Emkebpe waiting on the other side for me, so I walked out and he took my arm and we walked.

I noticed I was wearing a white dress. I started seeing my hubbie's cousin in her wedding dress. She was so happy and dancing and laughing (she's getting married in a few weeks actually). I turned to look at Emkebpe, and he smiled. Then everything changed to nighttime. In front of me was a water fountain running water long way. To my left corner, I saw the Moon bright as day, then I saw a lot of animals gathered around. It was like they were attending a ceremony and Emkebpe was like a father image to them. Then everyone got quiet and still.

Emkebpe came to me holding a bowl and gave it to me. I took it and inside was water with the Moon's reflection.

The water was white. I looked at everyone else. Emkebpe indicated for me to drink it, so I didn't hesitate and drank it. The moment I took my first sip, all the animals bowed down. Emkebpe smiled and bowed as well. The water was like air that naturally went inside. It felt more like I inhaled it. I suddenly felt very warm. The warmth got even more intense, and I saw myself expanding. I also felt grounded and more stable. I felt strong in my own energy like I was even more connected to my true self. Emkebpe took me and we walked back inside that white flame.

I asked if he needed or wanted anything in return and he replied, "No, but open your hands," I opened my left hand and he gave me a white rose. The rose went inside me, and within my own world, I saw white roses filling up the entire space. I thanked him and closed the ritual. This went very smoothly and quickly. Towards the end shared some insights about myself that have been dormant in some ways and showed me how to awaken them. I really felt that he was a fatherly entity. It was also revealed to me that he is also one of the best teachers of soul flames. Not in the sense of the element fire, but as the essence of an aspect of the soul which consists of flames. It can be seen in varieties of colours or be heard in different frequencies. However, the best way to delve deeper into that knowledge is through the element of water magic. This is already regarded as Advanced water magic or numerically 9. After graduating from Advanced water magic, the selected few who are suited to learn about the soul and its constitution are only allowed to enter this phase of learning/teaching apparently. He showed me the curriculum of this teaching and from what I understood, unless this is an area someone specializes in and already has advanced knowledge or their higher selves and spirit guides have guided them through, amateurs will not be able to comprehend this level of knowledge. That person just has to be wired that way from the get-go.

Warning

The Picatrix's talisman: The image of a dragon fighting with a man, The lord of this Mansion is written in front of this figure.
Agrippa's talisman: A dragon fighting with a man.
Bruno's image: A dragon fighting with a man.

According to the Picatrix, the twelfth Mansion Azarfa, can be used for the separation of two lovers.

Black magic can transform the **House of Peace and Love** into the **House of broken Peace and Love.**

There are thousands of ways to destroy love and peace, and black magicians can get tempted to try that. There are many ways to destroy a good marriage too with jealousy, possessiveness, unfaithfulness, disloyalty, mistrust, arguments, obsession, etc. The magicians may try to create talismans to create disharmony and other big problems for couples in love.

Emkebpe is a protector of sailors, but the magician, through negative influences from this Mansion, might try to do exactly the opposite, to use negative powers from the Moon in order to: destroy and sink ships and make sailors suffer.

13th Genius – Emcheba

Arabian Name: Azerut
Western Tradition: Iazeriel
The Picatrix's Talisman: A red wax image of a man with an erection desiring to be in coitus with a woman. A white wax image of a woman. These two images are facing each other and are wrapped in a piece of white silk. In whichever image the name of the desired person is written.
Agrippa's Talisman: Images of man in red wax and woman in white wax embracing
Bruno's Image: A stallion serving a mare, while a shepherd leans on his staff. His head is resting on both hands. He is looking on with a fixed expression
Emcheba is the head of the 13th Mansion: Alahue or Alhaire (Dog Star or Virgin's Wings)
The House of Longevity and Love: 4°17'09" Virgo - 17° 08'34" Virgo
Position of the 13th Mansion in the Moon Zone: It is mostly a watery part of the Moon

Emcheba portrays as a sage with grey hair and a long beard. This tall and handsome spirit likes to dress in shorts and a t-shirt or in any other modern or informal way. This genius sometimes appears accompanied by a very beautiful blonde female angel by his side. He is very friendly and lively. Emcheba brings fun, joy and satisfaction, and he likes to party.

Emcheba was traditionally recognized to be a teacher of sexual magic, especially effective for the "agreement of married couples and for dissolving charms against copulation". He can also help men who are not able to "come to women" and for the creation of love between opposite sexes. Like a few other heads of the Earth Zone, Emcheba is also a guardian of happiness in marriage. If the magician cannot find love or if there is no sex in marriage due to certain types of curses, Emcheba is the best spirit from the Moon to call for help in order to break that black magic.

Emcheba is also a teacher of beauty, so the magician can become remarkably handsome or beautiful with his help. Some of his subordinate spirits' role is to refresh nature and preserve its beauty. This genius can help magicians look youthful regardless of their age.

This genius can also tell many interesting stories about immortals, the people who have gained eternity through alchemical efforts, magical means and spiritual self-sacrifices.

Emcheba is the best expert of mummial magic and a master of all immortals from the Moon and Earth Zone. He closely cooperates with the following masters of mummial magic from the Earth Zone: Siges (7° Aquarius), Tabbata (10° Leo), Kirek (9° Virgo), Helali (4° Cancer) and Emfalion (5° Cancer). Franz Bardon has given a short description about how Emchebe can teach magicians to create their own mummies and how with their help they might carry through their "astro-magical pacts" without leaving any disadvantageous traces in Akasha. As this should be treated as very advanced magic, you should directly ask Emcheba for further instructions and explanations in this regard. The main point is that magicians' mummies may help them fulfil all of their wishes in all three planes. Additionally, Emcheba may disclose to the magician many mysteries related to Egyptian mummies. He can tell many forgotten and never before told stories about A'ah, Khons, Thoth and several other Egyptian Lunar gods and people who worshipped them.

This genius is probably the best Egyptologist in our part of the Universe, so ask this angel for help if you want to deepen your knowledge about Egyptian magic, history and culture.

Additional Observations Relevant to Emcheba's Teaching on Egyptian Lunar Gods

- A'ah (A'oh) was worshipped in Egypt some 5000 years ago. In later times, he was associated with Osiris or Thoth.
- Khons was particularly worshipped in Thebes. He was seen as a young king with the Moon symbol on his shaved head. He was called: Navigator, Creator of Destiny, Child, Full Moon, Powerful Young Man, and His Mother's Ox. Khons was also a protector of childbirth and a chronicler of the heavens and times. Khon's cult spread to other parts of Egypt. The Egyptians believed that Khons had power over all evil spirits. He became worshipped as an exorcist and healer. Sick people from all over Egypt and the neighbouring states went to Khons' temples to heal. One month was called in Egypt - pakhons - Month of Khons.
- Thoth was a god of the Moon, writing and magic. The Egyptians worshipped Thoth as the mightiest magician and the ruler of Divine words, secret formulae, rituals, evocations and magical protections. Thoth is also connected to the mystical "Book of Thoth" which is, according to many occultists, the biggest treasure of hermetic tradition with its 42 papyri of wisdom.

Evocation Experiences

Talerman

Emcheba was showing me pictures in a slideshow and sometimes I could hear his comments about them. In the beginning, the pictures were not so easy to see, but at the end, I could watch the slideshow very clearly. The pictures were of many things and symbols which were attributed to the Moon and there was also a lot of water in them: rivers, lakes, oceans, cups, and chalices. When I saw a few pictures of flowers, I heard this angel saying: "They are not only drinking when you are watering them, what they are then also doing is enjoying taking a shower".

Then he showed me a beautiful ancient map of the oceans and seas of the Moon Zone. He said that he could help me in love matters and gave me a rock crystal which had beautiful red light inside. He changed his subject to Egypt and then spoke enigmatically about an African tribe whose hero Cameon (or maybe spelt 'Kameon') had become a god after his death and gone on to live on the Moon.

Kadiliya

I was greeted by a funny-looking jester. He was silent. He took me to a big dark forest. We came to a castle with Emcheba's name on it. We went inside and I saw stairs going up. A red carpet rolled in front of me and there stood a tall man. I felt that he was very handsome even though I couldn't really see his face. He came and took me with him.

We started walking while introducing ourselves. Suddenly everything around us vanished and we were standing in the galaxy. We talked and exchanged ideas about magic. Then he turned around and I saw what he was wearing from the bottom up. I asked if this was his true form and he replied, "In a way yes." He then continued, "You seem very tired and you should rest. Come back tomorrow and we can continue our discussion." I agreed and left.

When I tried to evoke him again, I did see Emcheba, but he was far away. He turned away and started walking. I followed him and again I got distracted by some thoughts. I came back again hearing the voice, "Follow the jester." So I did and came back to the same dark forest, the same castle and I was greeted by Emcheba again. We talked and he shared that there were lots of things he wanted to teach me. We discussed the mummial-related magic, how it was never about actually bringing back the dead to life and how the significance of it was in the timeline itself (almost like preserving a timeline for the deceased).

As he went on about it, I noticed a sudden shift in sexual energy, which brought the idea that perhaps this spirit also deals with sexual magic. Furthermore, he shared his knowledge about ancient magic related to ancient and dead languages and why certain gods prefer to this day to use them. It is because of their resonances when vibrated in a certain way, but this can only be revealed or taught when Emcheba is evoked properly. He also started talking about the importance of entertainment and how through comedy, acting and singing, a magician can change big events and make big impacts in the world.

Warning

Black magic can turn the **House of Longevity and Love** into the **House of Pride**. Very successful, and beautiful, but self-centred and selfish magicians can come out as a result of such magic. As for other side-effects related to this Mansion, too much partying and entertainment can lead people to self-destruction if they do not know how or when to stop. Related to mummial magic, even though magicians' karma might not be so much affected by the potential misdeeds of their mummies, they may lose control over their mummies, which is a potential magical disaster.

14TH GENIUS – EZHOBAR

Arabian Name: Erdegel
Western Tradition: Ergediel
Ezhobar is the head of the 14th Mansion: Alchureth, Arimet, Azimeth, Althumech or Alcheymech
The House of Initiation: 17°08'34" Virgo - 0°0'0 Libra
Position of the 14th Mansion in the Moon Zone: Astral region
Talismans and Imagers: Presented in the 'Warning' section of this entry because they were traditionally used for malevolent purposes

Ezhobar is a very powerful, friendly and easygoing spirit. He often appears as an old man with a long white beard, white-tied knot hair and sunken eyes. He is like a Tao master dressed in a simple white shirt and trousers.

Archangels are rarely alone. Ezhobar is one of the main associates of Archangel Gabriel, so when magicians are working with Ezhobar, it is likely for them to see this archangel too. Ezhobar is one of Gabriel's main spirits, and as such he has always been by his side helping him in his missions with many unknown but also well-known people such as Mohammad, Joseph, Joshua, Daniel, Maria, Joan d'Arc, John Dee, Edward Kelley, etc. Some people cannot stand Gabriel's vibrations, so Ezhobar often comes to them instead.

Ezhobar is a guardian of all Moon gates. He is able to light the path of the Moon to true aspirants. This genius is able to see what is missing within the aspirants and to guide them gently to where they need to be when working with the Lunar magic. There are two main initiators into the Moon magic: Ebvap, the 1st genius and Ezhobar, the 14th genius. If the magician is a beginner, it is the best time to start with the Moon magic when the Moon is either in its 1st or 14th Mansion, with either Ebvap or Ezhobar.

Ezhobar can help the magician achieve astonishing results with the Moon magic. Franz Bardon has said that this genius may help the magician with levitation, changing the polarity of gravity, interpretation of Lunar symbols and comprehension of the laws of the Moon sphere. When the magician meets Ezhobar, this would practically mean that their Lunar magic would become easier and more efficient than before. Ezhobar will help if all your efforts to achieve success with the Moon magic would fail.

Magicians who choose to delve deep into the subconscious and excel at dream magic might find it very beneficial to evoke Ezhobar, as he is one of the main kings of dreams from the Moon Zone. Without the Moon, no being from the Earth would be able to sleep. Magicians may sleep with seals of Ezhobar under their pillows to ward off nightmares and fear of the dark. This genius inspires humanity when it sleeps at night with positive influences from the Moon. Dreams are often easily forgotten, so Ezhobar can also help to remember them. Ezhobar also teaches how to dream walk too.

Ezhobar can also tell many interesting and so far untold stories about how the Moon can be interpreted in divination.

Ezhobar is a master of imagination, fantasy and illusions. Astral parts of the Moon are mostly as real and genuine as our world is. Certain phenomena on the Moon might also appear to be illusionary, but that can also be said for the planet Earth (as in the case of fata morgana which comes into view due to the refraction of the light). Ezhobar helps the magician distinguish reality from illusion. Many intelligent geniuses of the Moon from time to time enjoy creating purposeful illusions. Such illusions are often powered by hidden mysteries and messages. With direct access to the astral realm which is less exposed to the law of gravity, they have more opportunities to play with levitation, dematerialization and other phenomena. Nevertheless, some lunar teachers may purposely put unreal pictures before magicians whose task would then be to recognize the illusion and dematerialize it by their own willpower. For the above reasons, there are many illusions on the astral Moon, which makes some people falsely believe that the whole astral region is an illusion.

Ezhobar can help you understand and interpret angelic and prophetic messages properly, especially when they come from archangels. The Koran itself was influenced by three sources: Archangel Gabriel's messages, the Djin's communication and Mohamed's own interpretations of received messages.

This angel can also help you to master the art of channelling. Safe travels on land, water and air are guaranteed by Ezhobar as well. Finally, he is also one of the best teachers of water magic in the Moon Zone.

Additional Observations Relevant to Ezhobar's Teachings

Archangel Gabriel

- Gabriel is an extremely intelligent and powerful angel. He is usually described as tall and thin and dressed in silvery or black clothes. He sometimes holds a lily as a sign of cleanliness. Gabriel may also, albeit quite rarely, appear with strange Cherubim characteristics (Muhammad describes him as an archangel with "140 pairs of wings").

- Ceremonial magicians often connect this archangel with the element of water. They invoke Gabriel to protect their magical circle from its western side where his chalice is placed. Gabriel's sigil contains angelic signs for power, persistence, goodness, mercy, hope and humanity. It can be used for: evoking any other lunar spirits, creativity, dream work and accessing the subconscious.
- Gabriel is a guardian of the door between life and death. He is said to be heard saying: "Don't worry, I can always provide you a new body on the Earth if you want another one."
- Sandalphon and Gabriel cooperate closely about all important things concerning the Earth and the Moon.
- When Archangel Gabriel does not show, one of his subordinates who looks like an old wise ascendant master shows up and opens the gateways to Yesod.
- Any beloved deceased pets are often led towards the gates of light with Gabriel's assistance, but often those pets end up becoming Gabriel's spirit animals that help around in Lunar spheres.
- Hazel Raven, the author of "The Angel Bible" suggests people to use etheric oils of coriander, mimosas or narcissus if they want to get in touch with Archangel Gabriel in dreams.
- Milton sees Archangel Gabriel as a commander of the Eden angelic guardians.

The Moon in Divination

The Moon is a favourable symbol in dreams. It predicts sudden luck, success in love and the end of troubles. The Waxing Moon in dreams is good for traders, farmers and lovers, while the Full Moon sometimes predicts marriage. The Full Moon in the coffee ground indicates a future love relationship which will last longer if it is followed by some other good signs. The Waxing Moon in the coffee ground talks about new beginnings and projects, while the Waning Moon predicts some limitations and obstacles. One light circle around the Moon predicts rain; one large circle indicates heavy rain; several concentric circles announce bad weather for a long time; the light-yellow color of the Moon predicts nice weather in summer, but cold weather in winter; if the Full Moon is pale and surrounded by clouds, it talks about humidity; and the Red Moon predicts windy weather.

Illusion, Memories, Imagination and Allegory

Dion Fortune has said that Yesod treasures pictures from the mundane sphere created by human beings from time immemorial. The magician is in a situation to open up that treasure, enjoy what it is inside and make use of such immense heritage. William Grey has noticed that astral Yesod is also a sphere of allegories, allusions and euphemisms, which are the truths but adaptable to our capabilities to understand them. Imagination is our reflection of other worlds' realities. Spiritual sciences are based on otherworldly images and are attractive to imaginative people. The magician with imagination is sure to contact many spirits from other worlds.

Channelled Materials

Gareth Knight has estimated in his book "Magical pictures and imaginations" that charlatans, tricksters and neophytes give 98% of channelled materials.

Evocation Experiences

Talerman

Ezhobar told me that my will must be in the control over my emotions all the time when I am on the Moon. If the will loses control, my mind would bring me back to Earth instantly.

He said that important planetary spirits are generally familiar with human problems and that they appreciate when a magician from our world would appear in the astral world. Then he continued, "When you are on other planets with your body in the right frequencies, your teachers, guides, guardians, heads and their subordinate spirits will know who and where you are from, but all other random spirits around you will take you as one of their own kind, unless you tell them that you are not. If you for some reason want them to respect you, you can tell them that you are a mortal being from the Earth and still alive. It is useful to say that to them if you get lost and ask them to find a way to a particular place or spirit. If they do not respect you, they will not take you seriously there and probably just ignore you."

Then we started talking about Archangel Gabriel. When I acknowledged that it had taken me at least one year to understand a message from Gabriel and that even to that day I was not sure if I understood it properly, Ezhobar told me that archangels' messages are always powerful and often unforgettable, but also sometimes hard to understand.

He then also said that many messages which had been prescribed to Gabriel had actually been delivered to people by the Djin. Ezhobar then said that the Djin is a "fake Gabriel". He confirmed to me that Mohamed himself had moments when he believed that the Djin had spoken to him. Once Mohamed was so terrified by the Djin's voice that he wanted to commit suicide but was prevented by Archangel Gabriel who appeared at the last moment to save his life. When I asked Ezhobar if I ever had met the Djin, he told me that I probably had a few times. "Your soul needs to be clean at the moment you want to see Gabriel," he said and continued, "Otherwise, you might meet the Djin instead."

𝒦ADILIYA

I cleared the room and asked for Gabriel's aid and protection from all types of negative influences. I began my ritual, at first nothing happened, but soon I came to a crisp forest with a river running along my side. There were small rocks piled on top of each other by the water, so out of curiosity, I went to the water to see if there was anything inside. I saw some strange-looking white fish, but suddenly a man's face appeared in the water. He was smiling a lot looking at me. When I turned around there was no one, but when I turned back he was still in the water's reflection. I asked if he was Ezhobar and he replied, "Yes".

I introduced myself and he said he knew who I was the moment I arrived. I asked him why he was in the reflection and he said, "Because you're missing a few steps to come to my realm." He was still smiling. I asked him where he was, and he said, "Home!" He asked me if I would like to come and I yes "Yes" with excitement. He said, "Okay, I'll teach you how. It's very simple, don't overthink it. You see where I'm at? Well, just walk towards it." I think I knew what he meant but I couldn't really say, so I followed my intuition and walked towards him. The image that I was seeing was the image I walked into. Then I was there. He laughed and said, "Often people get confused because they're using their logical minds. But you're in the Lunar realm, you must let go of the material." He sat down in a meditation pose. I asked him, "Did you know Franz Bardon?" He looked at me with a big smile, laughed and said, "Did I? Oh yes! When he came, he was so eager to learn, very enthusiastic and ready to learn. By the time he came here he let go of a lot of his pride and what he thought he knew. A very good student indeed." I smiled feeling like I was there witnessing it. He said, "I want to teach you something about lunar magic. I see that you have a lot of water, so this will be very useful knowledge for you."

He then started using his hands to pull the water out of the river using gestures and I immediately followed him or copied him. I was able to pull the water out too. He continued while focusing on the water. "You see, lunar water is very special. You can drink it, use it for healing, use it to cleanse, use it to fulfill desires, but out of all, I'm going to show you something different." He was holding the water in front of his sacral chakra, so was I. He then pulled it up towards his third eye and closed his eyes. I did the same but I felt something strange. I felt a connection with the water, like communicating, but it was communicating with my subconscious. I heard him saying, "Now, while you're feeling that connection, go deep inside yourself. What do you want to know and see?" He then pushed the water a little out and pulled it in front of him and made it a square-like TV. I did the same. He told me to project what I want to know into that screen. I tried and my head started to hurt. He said, "You're trying too hard, breathe and relax. Let your mind go and let your heart be silent. Allow the soul to connect". Then the screen in front of me was a moving picture of a pitch-pouring white substance. It was thick and shiny. It eventually filled the whole screen. Then bubbles formed and writing appeared. (It's only relevant to me).

My head started to hurt again and I heard Ezhobar say, "Don't try too hard, there is no need. Be gentle, let the force dissolve," and I did as he said. All my anxieties and fears just vanished somewhere. Then the screen started to fill up with air bubbles like raindrops. I could even hear the rain. The bubbles then started to connect with each other and they made another screen which was crystal clear. In the background I heard Ezhobar, "Do not be afraid of what you will see," and I saw Metatron's cube forming from a single line. Then it changed into a red rectangular door, and within the rectangle, there was a black circle. The circle seemed like it was moving. I turned to Ezhobar and telepathically told him that I might need to go inside that door. He smiled and replied, "Go, I will be here waiting, you are safe and well protected." I felt like I needed to hear that. I felt my heart thump but I pushed it through and walked to the door. As I got closer to it, my clothes faded away. I soon became completely naked. I gave a final look at Ezhobar and walked into the black circle. Everything felt like pulling me, like a big force pulling my entire being forwards. I almost felt like being squeezed, a little uncomfortable I'd say. Time also felt irrelevant. Things were squeezed like there was gravity but also weren't. Then everything became white. That black circle turned into a white circle. I stopped all of a sudden. I looked around and everything was white. I took a step. Grass grew instantly on the floor. I took another step and more greens flourished. I even felt the texture on the bottom of my feet. I kept walking until a single line of green grew to form a path.

I took that path and came to a giant huge tree. I could see the roots of the tree. They were red like blood. The leaves on the tree were golden white with an aura. I then saw something above the tree, it looked like the Sun. As I got closer to the tree, I noticed that it was split into two from up and forming into one from the middle and down to the base. In the centre, there were writings that were almost invisible but also strange and old so I couldn't read them. But I felt like I should be able to. I reminded myself not to overthink too much, so I didn't try too hard. I took a step back and suddenly something entered my feet. The roots from the tree went inside my feet from the base. I stared at the tree for a while not really understanding it but knowing that it was part of me.

I could hear Ezhobar talk in the background, "You've walked through the door that you've been afraid of, it was also something you've been seeking. Now you have it. You now know the path to this place, you can visit it anytime you like. You can learn much more from here." Then I walked out. Ezhobar got up and looked very happy. He told me to come back anytime I liked. I asked if I could share any of this with anyone he said, "That is up to you." He told me I may leave now, but he would be here if I needed him in the future. I asked him if he wanted anything in return – he said no. He turned around, laughed loudly, waved at me, and finally turned into hundreds of white birds and butterflies and vanished. I thanked him and came out.

I forgot to mention one thing about Ezhobar, his teachings on Lunar water is very interesting and useful knowledge. If anyone wants to learn more about it, or even about the water element, he can definitely help with that.

Warning

Picatrix's talisman: The image in red wax of a dog with his own tail held in his mouth.
Agrippa's talisman: A dog biting his tail.
Bruno's image: A man holding a dog suspended by its tail, with the dog biting its own hind foot.

Traditionally, the pentacles of this genius were used for divorce and separation of the man from the woman. Black magic can turn the **House of Initiation** can be turned to the **House of Failed Initiation**.

15ᵀᴴ Genius – Emnepe

Arabian Name: Achalich
Western Tradition: Atliel
The Picatrix's Talisman: Figure of a seated man, holding scrolls in his hands
Agrippa's Talisam: A man sitting and writing letters.
Bruno's Image: A man sitting, reading and who is a messenger
Emnepe is the head of the 15th Mansion: Agrapha or Algrapha
House of Divine Love: 0°0'0" - 12°51'26" Libra
Position of the 15th Mansion in the Moon Zone: The highest realm of the Moon Zone, Akasha Principle of the Moon, Yod of the Moon, close to Shaddai El Chai

Emnepe is both a scholar and a priest. He has been seen as a male spirit dressed in a white collar shirt and brown pants with suspenders, but when he is in his temple, he is dressed all in black. When he is not in the temple, he is most probably to be found reading books in his library. He was depicted as a reader in the talismans from the Picatrix, Agrippa and Giordano Bruno. Franz Bardon also connects Emnepe to reading but "in the Akasha principle." Emnepe comes across as a very friendly spirit, eager to teach in the areas of Akasha, Divine Names and Divine Love. This genius welcomes his guests with a cup of tea or coffee. Make sure to also offer something in return. Many Lunar spirits and angels can be seen with tea or coffee in their hands while they are teaching and learning.

Emnepe is one of the mightiest guardians of Akasha from the Moon Zone. In his region, there are many: Akashic libraries, bookstores, schools, temples, archives and workshops. Emnepe can teach about how to read mental, astral and physical events in Akasha. He can guide you to see the past and future of any person or nation. Additionally, he can also teach the magician how to influence all events from Akasha. In this respect, he closely cooperates with Achaiah and Hahahel, the two Shemhamforosh angels, and the following heads of the Earth Zone: Belifares, Badet, Jrachro, Bruahi, Ygarimi, Akahimo, Aragor, Milon and Charonthona.

Emnepe's knowledge and wisdom regarding the Divine names and their associating attributes of the Moon are vast. This genius can instruct how to connect to the Moon, enter the Moon Zone and evoke Lunar spirits with the help of Shaddai El Chai. God's names and attributes are the mightiest protectors of all celestial bodies and galaxies, while the Divine realms of each star and planet are ruled by one of God's names. Moreover, Angelic realms of the Moon are given to the Cherubim and Gabriel, while its Divine region is governed by Shaddai El Chai (Shaddai El means "Mighty Lord," and Chai means, "Life," and his full name is "Mighty Lord of Life"). Emnepe can also show how to rely on Shaddai El Chai when we want to: invoke a certain quality of Yesod, affect materialization, and understand Lunar principles on life revivals. According to Emnepe, all genii and other spirits from the Moon can be evoked in the name of Shaddai El Chai. Not all people are equally attracted to the name Shaddai El Chai, so this genius can also give you advice about what other Divine names you might use in conjurations of Lunar gods and other spirits instead.

Emnepe can also encourage the magician to get in touch with the following 8 Shemhameforash angels who are closely related to the Moon magic: Nemamiah, Jeialel, Harahel, Mizrael, Umabel, Jah-Hel, Amianuel and Mehiel. He is also a special link to those 8 angels' respective God's names: Tara, Pora, Bogo, Deos, Deos, Aris, Zeut and Kalo.

Emnepe's subordinate spirits are mostly priests and scholars. Like all other lunar heads, Emnepe may go wherever he wants, but he prefers to stay in his library, which is in Akasha, near Shaddai El Chai, in the highest realm of the Moon Zone. Emnepe's habitat is in the region of the Moon which in cabalistic terminology is called Atziluth of Yesod or the Yod of the Moon. In Emnepe's region, the magician may see how the first principals of all Lunar bodies are being created throughout the Universe. Besides the Moon, Emnepe may also teach magicians about God's powers and attributes of all other moon-like bodies around the Universe. Emnepe can reveal all secrets about relations between the Moon and all other planets and stars.

In the faculties of Divine love and virtues, Emnepe shares that the magician can work together with the following masters from the Earth Zone: Ylemis (29° Pisces), Afrei (12° Libra), Anemalon (9° Leo), Kalote (16° Cancer) and Koreh (17° Aquarius). He believes in "teamwork," so he closely cooperates with many great teachers from the Earth, the Moon and all other planets from our Solar system.

Emnepe is also one of the strongest guardians of love and friendship. He is a special patron of good neighbourhoods, so if there is any problems with the neighbours, the magician may ask him for help. According to the Picatrix and medieval European sources (such as Agrippa and Giordano Bruno), this angel is useful for the acquisition of friendship, goodwill, and anything that pertains to friends and lovers.

In the Picatrix, this genius can also help with lost treasures. Treasure hunting was one of the favourite magical disciplines from the past and it was never taken lightly since it was proven to be potentially quite dangerous.

Emnepe is one of the few Lunar genii who do not help travelers, so do not call him for help for that purpose. When the Moon is in the 15th Mansion it is recommended to stay at home: studying, reading, meditating, cleaning, help friends and family. Emnepe once said, "Clean house, Clean mind." When it comes to cleanliness, he can show you many ways how to enjoy housework (vacuum cleaning, washing dishes, etc). Magicians, inspired by this genius, will start looking at their house works as a special magical task and not as a boring discipline. This head also encourages magicians to keep their magical spaces and tools clean.

Additional observations relevant to Emnepe's teachings

God's Names

Each planet was created by some special word uttered by God. The cabalist William Grey says that God said in Kether "Let it be light!" and in Yesod, "Let it be Life!"

Shaddai El Chai

In the magical cabala, Shaddai El Chai is connected to Archangel Gabriel and all lunar genii and angels. Dion Fortune has written in her novel "Magic of the Moon" how she evoked Archangel Gabriel by the "holy name of Shaddai El Chai". Evoking angels and archangels in the name of Shaddai El Chai is a usual practice in the magical cabala. What makes Dion Fortune different is that she also wrote how she had summoned Egyptian lunar gods using the name Shaddai El Chai. Dion Fortune's syncretic approach could be sometimes workable in practice and sometimes not. Many advanced magicians do not like to mix up different systems when they start their rituals. Many magicians who do not belong to Judeo-Christian traditions would certainly not evoke Lunar gods with Shaddai El Chai. Some pagan magicians have already established a few non-Judeo-Christian methods of conjurations. For instance, New-Platonic God's name for the Moon is Aigle Trisagia – Threefold Light, while the Hermetic organization "Aurum Solis" uses God's name IAO for the highest sphere of the Moon, and Theonoemenos, Armateon, Kamaira and Ierochos for the four lower Lunar regions.

Evocation Experiences

Talerman

I saw Emnepe how he was performing liturgy in his temple together with his priests. They were all dressed in black with hoods covering most of their faces. The temple was made of large blocks of marble in silver and black, which seems to be used in Lunar architecture quite often as they are some of the favourite colours of the Moon. They preached about the Divine virtues of the Moon. I was stunned because each movement and step they made in their ritual seemed to be in accordance with the Divine Providence and that God was directly answering their questions. I had a feeling that they were directly communicating with God.

In the temple, there were also a few people who had just passed away. Emenpe and his priests were helping them regain confidence and find new directions. Death is probably the biggest shock to all people, no matter how spiritual they might have been while alive. I saw how Emnepe was helping them adjust to new circumstances. In this temple, I was also in a position to be in the company of those people who had died. I could feel their despair, anxiety, worries and sorrow. They were together with one of the greatest genii from the Moon Zone, which means that they deserved it to be there by their good deeds and good karma. They actually belong to a group of very lucky people, and yet they were shocked and not prepared to die at all.

I might have also seen my own future to witness my own transition when I die. I do not know that for sure because I was too shocked by this experience to think about anything.

KADILIYA

I started by sending off a vibration that carried his name. Very quickly I saw a snake slithering in front of me in a desert-like place and it lead me to a sand dune, but I felt this was the wrong place. I said that I was looking for Emnepe of the Lunar realm and then the whole scenery changed. It gave a Mars sense, so I thought I was on Geburah.

After a little while, I found myself standing on a sandy beach and the same snake was slithering in front again, indicating me to follow and I did. The snake went into the ocean and I walked in. At first, I was swimming, but the snake went all the way down so I followed. I was able to breathe and walk on the bottom. We came to a house with pearl lamp posts. There was a doormat that said in arched style "Emnepe" and I looked up. At the door, it also said the same thing. The snake went inside through this little snake door (doggy door except for snakes).

I knocked and rang the doorbell but the door opened on it on and I heard "Come in." I walked in and it was like a cabin with a fireplace. There was a long table in the centre, and at the end of it was a man in his 40s sitting and reading a book. He had a candle as his lamp, but it wasn't a regular candle. There were shiny things flying around creating white light. I asked him if he was Emnepe and he said, "Yes". I asked him what he was reading and he showed it to me. The writings in the book were constantly fading and reappearing. The book had olive-green and white colours and an aura over it. I told him who I was and he just looked at me. He asked if I wanted to take a look around his place because he had interesting things that I might like. I said, "Yes please." He started showing me around and soon we were surrounded by books, tons of books on tons of shelves. I said, "You sure read a lot", and he said, "Oh, haha, yes and no. Most of these books belong to students who come at my door. You see?", and he showed me books of other magicians' names on them. He continued, "These books will only open to the right person at the right time." Then I saw three books inside a cabinet; one at the centre was peculiar: it was big, shiny, and it kept jumping. Emnepe said, "Oh, that book is weird. It jumps when it senses a certain person. I still haven't figured out the difference, ignore it". I asked what the book was about and he said, "Um, not yet. Perhaps later when the opportunity comes I can show it to you.".It was something advanced. Then I got closer to the book and it gave off a lavender and citrus scent and purple and green aura. I told that to Emnepe and he turned around and said, "Did it now? Interesting," and he left it as that. He said, "Come along, let's find your book."

We went down and up and all around the house, but we didn't find my book. He kept murmuring something to himself, and then I saw a book that had my name on it but it didn't open and he said, "Oh, you can put that back." I said, "But it has got my name on it", and he replied, "Yes, but something has changed in you, didn't it? So this belonged to the past you, not you now, you know what I mean?" I was a little confused and he said, "Look, who did you visit last before you came to me? Well, since then something has changed and that's why this book won't open right now. As you can see, your name is fading." And I looked at the book and my name was fading and also changing. It was weird. Then he seemed a little frustrated and said, "I can't find your book, let me hold your hands, and I gave him my hands. We sat at the table and he closed his eyes. I started to worry because what would that mean now? My book that had my name is fading away. Then he said, "Come back again tomorrow during the day, I'll have something for you", so he sent me off.

I went back the next morning and found him. I asked about the book situation and he told me he didn't find it. He shared that it was due to certain changes that occurred recently that my "old" book was there but technically it's no longer mine and I need to look elsewhere to find it. And apparently, when certain magicians/adepts gain certain wisdom they can somewhat rewrite history. There are many stages to that rewriting aspect and it's not easily done, but it is achievable.

Before I left, he asked a favour of me which was to lead "others" to his region. When I asked him how, he simply said, "Just like the way you found me by following the snakes!" He also later revealed to me that my book might be in the Grand Library.

At another time I had a dream of sitting with Emnepe by the Lunar oceans on a stone bench watching the waves go by while being surrounded by the most beautiful blue glistening sand. It was very intimate like sitting with someone you truly love and feel safe with. He shared his stories of how he was stationed in this particular Lunar region and his predecessors were the ones who had been my teachers a long time ago. I asked him if he knew where they were now and he said he didn't. However, I would meet them again on my journeys.

We discussed rage, death and acceptance. Simply put, rage for everyone is different and stems from different aspects of the soul's choices they make after incarnation either on Earth or other planetary systems. For instance, if a soul chooses the Earth to incarnate for whatever reason or purpose, a veil gets put in the subconscious for growth purposes. However, with the forgetting, the soul starts to feel resentment. That resentment comes from a place of the unknown, so it lacks self-awareness. The seed of rage comes from not knowing and forgetting. That being said, life on Earth is very polarized. It has its own way of balancing. Thus knowledge and teachings are out there for everyone and can provide the pathway to awakening. The veil of forgetting is not absolute either. It is very fluid and it is like that for a reason. If it was absolute, then remembering would be impossible. After all, the Earth is a school. All life on the Earth is intimately connected to the Divine, thus everything that is alive or has a vibration can feel or hear deep within itself that voice of truth. Ultimately, everything looks for and seeks out the very light of truth. If one chooses to hold on to that vibration, then the vibration will open catalysts and pathways for that being to grow and connect with their Divinity. The higher densities one can reach, the more polarity becomes irrelevant in the next octave of learning. Emnepe's words regarding death were "It is merely a graduation from an octave. As polarization decreases so do the concept of death." Acceptance can be perceived as music. Emnepe says, "Acceptance and music are alike. You don't necessarily have to understand each instrument that is creating sounds. You listen and feel the vibrations and you accept it if it resonates with you. When you watch the ocean waves silently, do you reject them or do you appreciate them for what they are? When one embraces and truly resonances and can feel the waves, there is often a sense of relief, as if all the burdens have dissolved. You feel lighter and one with the element. When one rejects the waves or even struggles to watch them, they may feel overwhelmed as if they are drowning. That feeling becomes much denser which in turn might make them want to leave the ocean. Acceptance is very similar in that way. As you learn more about yourself and grow, the more mature and patient you become and lessons become a little easier to accept." As he continued with his teachings, a sense of my own existence coming to an end washed all over me, but it did not feel foreign, as if I had done it many times. It felt neutral. This spirit has so much to share and teach.

Warning

Black magic can turn the **House of Divine Love** into the **House of Depression.** The Picatrix suggests that Achalich wrath is useful: for impeding travellers so that they are unable to go on journeys, to separate husbands and wives so that they never join with each other, to place discord between friends and allies, to scatter enemies from their area, and for the destruction of the reputation of a family house of your enemies. Some western grimoires tell that he may go even so far as to make people "destroy each others' houses" and steal "each others' wives."

Related to dangers from treasure hunting, in one instance, Solomon caught a female demon, Onoskelis, who appeared in a shape of a beautiful woman with the legs of a mule. She told Solomon that she lived in a cave and that she helped men to discover lost treasures, but then she would drive them mad and choke them off. She used to travel at the time of the Waning Moon and was closely connected to the constellation of Capricorn. She was said to be prevented in her misdeeds by God's name JAHVEH. If you ever happened to encounter some demonic creatures like Onoskelis during your treasure hunt, remember to ask Emnepe for help!

Magicians may start losing interest in life slowly progressing towards apathy as a counter-effect of the Moon magic. They might feel that the world they live in presents a lower kind of existence compared to some higher realms. If you start despising your earthly existence and neglecting your mundane reality, ask Emnepe to restore full strength through meditation on Shaddai El Chai. Emnepe encourages everyone to express and live life to the fullest towards the highest ideals which they might possibly reach. When meditation on Shaddai El Chai, Emnepe will remind the magician about the beauty and meaning of life.

16ᵀᴴ Genius – Echotasa

Arabian Name: Acubene
Western Tradition: Azeruel
The Picatrix's Talisman: On a plate of silver the figure of a man is fashioned seating on a throne and carrying a scale in his hands
Agrippa's Talisman: A man sitting on a chair, holding a balance in his hands
Bruno's Image: A merchant holding silver scales in his hand, while the hand of another man is counting money out to him
Echotasa is the head of the 16th Mansion: Azubene or Ahubene (Horns of Scorpio)
House of Protection and Wealth: 12°51'26" - 25°42'52" Libra
Position of the 16ᵗʰ Mansion in the Moon Zone: Astral part of the Moon. Even though it is not that difficult to evoke the genius of this Mansion, interestingly enough it is quite difficult to reach the realm where he lives

Echotasa is a tall spirit with gray short hair, a small goatee and a small white moustache. He was seen wearing a hat and a golden robe. According to Franz Bardon, it should not be that difficult to evoke Echotasa since he is "a very benevolent intelligence, who will be pleased to give the mature magician any kind of assistance". His faculties focus on: Lunar protection, banishment, exorcisms, symbolisms, hidden mysteries, and much more. In his free time, he likes to play chess and board games.

Echotasa is rarely seen alone. His subordinate spirits are described as crusaders, angels, psychopomps, and blessed souls. Often enough they are the ones that will appear and lead the magician to him. Those spirits reside in one of Echotasa's most beautiful regions on the Moon. However, it is not easy to get to it. For instance, old Egyptians thought that the Moon was populated by just people, while old Slovakians and Latvians saw it as a sphere of blessed souls. Each of their souls had to pass over a celestial bridge to reach the desired destination on the Moon, but their journey could take a long time. Many of them climbed up high and slippery celestial mountains in order to reach their heavens. Some were guided by psychopomps who resided in that region of the Moon. Echotasa can be called upon if the magician gets lost on their way to the Moon and even elsewhere. The astral parts of the Moon are good to visit if one wants to reach peace, become lucid and discover some deeper secrets of the soul and mind.

Echotasa was also traditionally asked for help with making money and liberating captives from incarceration. This genius may help the magician become a good merchant and have good financial results in trade. According to the modern astrologer Christopher Warnock, this Mansion "is superb for trade and business and indicates a positive answer to questions concerning wealth and prosperity".

Being one of the masters of protection against negative spirits, Echotasa is quite similar to Emvatibe, the head of the 4th Mansion. However, while Emvatibe protects against malevolent people, Echotasa mostly guards against negative spirits. Franz Bardon has said that taking control over all negative spirits of the Moon Zone is possible with Echotasa's help. In other words, when encountering malevolent people call for Emvatibe, but when under attack by malevolent spirits call for Echotasa! Many malevolent spirits of the Moon are good at disguising and pretending that they are benevolent, but Echotasa helps the magician recognize their tricks. Echotasa will typically suggest the magician learn protection magic according to their own religious background. For instance, if the magician is of Christian background, Echotasa may reveal many untold secret stories about how Jesus Christ battled demons. If the magician has a background in Islam, Buddhism, Taoism, Judaism, or any other religious or spiritual tradition, Echotasa can teach and show how to fight malevolent spirits accordingly. Moreover, he can also reveal great methods against malevolent spirits which are not a part of any religious or magical traditions.

Echotasa can teach you how to perform an exorcism. Malevolent spirits from the Moon almost never possess a person completely, but from time to time they can cause: illnesses, inner suffering, discordance, fights, arguments, separations, divorces, ends of friendships, psychosis and obsessions.

Echotasa can instruct the magician how to create excellent Moon amulets and talismans for protective purposes or for attraction of good Lunar influences.

This spirit is one of the greatest protectors for pedestrians and he is a guardian of all who travels on land, but it is not ideal to call for his help if one is travelling by ship or aeroplane. Like every other protective Lunar spirit, Echotasa encourages the magician to stay at home when the weather is bad if s/he has nothing to do outside.

Additional observations relevant to Echotasa's teachings

Christ as a Protector

Just like in the Bible, many other stories have also described Christ as a superb persecutor of evil spirits. All spirits in the sky, above the earth and within the earth were said to bow to him and he was said to chase away devils with his finger. He transferred his power of exorcism to his 12 apostles, then to each of his 72 students and finally to all people who believed in him. In his last speech, Jesus said that people who believed in him would be followed by many wonders, and one of them would be the knowledge to expel devils (Mk 16:17).

Protection from Malevolent Lunar Influences

You may use the Banishing Hexagram of the Moon in order to banish malevolent spirits. While drawing this hexagram on the floor or in the air, focus on Shaddai El Chai, Alim or Ararita. You may write one or all of their names too. Ask Christ, Shaddai El Chai, Archangel Gabriel, IHOVA, ELOHIM and ADONAI for help when there is an alarming situation. If you worship other deities connected to the Moon, like Diana, Selena or Hecate, call them for help instead. Whomever you choose to ask for help, be sure in advance that you have good relations with them and that they can hear you too. Seconds often decide upon life and death.

Identification of Malevolent Spirits

Archangel Sandalphon forced one female demon to tell him what names she had used to scare people and she mentioned them not less than 17: Abeko, Abito, Amizo, Batna, Ejlo, Ita, Izorpo, Kali, Kea, Kokos, Lilith, Odam, Partasa, Patrota, Podo, Satrina and Talto. The Solomonic magical cycle tells about the magical law according to which each spirit has to tell his or her true identity after being asked for it the third time. Enepsigos is one of the most terrible lunar demons. After Solomon caught her, she introduced herself to him twice as a goddess. But the third time she appeared as a demonic woman with two heads. Solomon forced her to a divine future. She told him that the Persians, Medians and Babylonians would destroy the Jerusalem

Temple, after which the demons would be released from their chains, but would be caught again by God's son whose name is Emmanuel.

Lunar Amulets

The Old Testament Book of Isaiah (3:18) condemned women who wore the lunar amulets, but in practice, people continued to use them anyway and even put them around their animals' necks. Agrippa has said in "Occult Philosophy" (II, 22) that Lunar stones could serve as amulets or talismans depending on the goal. The same goes for silver rings. The most efficient lunar amulets and talismans are mentioned in the "Greater Solomon Key" and in some other magical books.

Exorcism

The French exorcist Father Tonquedec has said, "A very few are possessed by Devil, but unfortunate spirits are in legions."

EVOCATION EXPERIENCES

TALERMAN

When I evoked Echotasa for the first time, I had to fight my way through to him, passing through different tunnels, jumping over high walls and climbing up slippery hills, which all lasted for about two hours, and though I finally did establish the contact with him, I was not so sure how he looked like because, besides him, there were also several other spirits involved in my evocation. Among them, one corpulent, powerful, strong, but also a very friendly black woman, showed me the way to a house where Echotasa lives. Even though I was not sure if it was him whom I saw there, I clearly heard his voice telling me that he could help me banish malevolent spirits, especially those among them who prevent people from gaining wealth. Then, I suddenly saw a few buses and trains passing by and heard Echotasa telling me that their passengers had his blessings for a safe journey. He said he is a special protector of all possible crossroads. He told me, "If you have problems with traffic, I will help you cross the street safely."

He also showed me and explained the rules of a very interesting astronomical Lunar board game, which also seems to be very popular on the Moon and quite simple to play.

Interestingly, the last time I evoked Echotasa, during the time while I have been writing this book, he asked me to play chess with him. In order to reach him, I again had to climb up to the top of a very tall lighthouse first, but I was not at all afraid of falling down. While I was climbing up and wondering why I was so brave, I heard Echotasa telling me, "Why should you be afraid, even if you fall down, you know how to fly!"

KADILIYA

I was floating somewhere and I looked around and spotted a lake. I saw a shore nearby, so I swam my way up until I reached the beach. A white dove flew to me and landed on the ground. I noticed something tucked away around one of its legs, so I picked it up and there was a small scroll. I opened the scroll and letters written in fountain pen started to appear. It said, "Isis: Follow the trees till the end". Then the bird flew away.

I started walking along the trees and noticed they were in a single line. Then I came to the end and saw a man wearing white trousers and holding a pitcher waiting for me. I came up to him and he greeted me. He asked if I would like a drink. I said yes, and he poured me something. I took a sip and it tasted sweet (but Lunar water sweet) with a hint of black tea. I asked if he was

Echotasa and he said no, but he would take me to him. We walked and came to a bamboo gate. As we were entering, I saw a lot of young girls lined up holding buckets. They were all smiling and laughing. As soon as we entered, I got water poured onto me by those girls and I was completely drenched.

I stood there in shock and surprise, and I laughed. I couldn't believe that I was wet! Then I slowly gathered myself and started walking. A group of little girls, maybe 7 or 8 of them, ran up to me and threw a whole bunch of flower petals on me. Now not only I was wet, but I also got flower petals stuck all over me and I smelled like flowers. I wiped my face and cleared my eyes from the petals and I looked up, everyone was laughing and cheering. It was actually hilarious.

Then that guy who had been with me before came up to me and I said, "Is this normal? It's nice of you to stay really far away from me when it happened!" He laughed and replied, "Yes, this is normal. May we continue?" I replied yes. At this point, I was walking carefully wondering what would happen next. Then I saw more kids running towards me. I got a little scared but they were holding something as they were running. I thought they were balloons. A kid came up to me and gave me a long stick with a bubble on top. Inside it was a small goldfish swimming. Then the kid ran off with others. I thanked him. I was just glad it wasn't some other surprise.

Surrounding us there were lots of houses which were white but with giant traditional doors. I thought to myself, "I guess this is where they live". Then we came to a house passing its gates. I saw a golden shimmer that said, 'Echosata' and it vanished. We came to the front yard where there was a big sandbox for zen meditation. I noticed that at the centre the sand was moving and shifting. Symbols were constantly shifting and changing into something different, but they had a pattern if you observe it carefully. That man who had been with me told me to wait there and he left. I thanked him and waited.

Out of curiosity, I went near the sand and it quickly changed into a triskele symbol. When I moved it away, it would disappear and go back to its original pattern. But when I got close enough, it would change back to the triskele symbol. I thought it was strange. Then a man approached me from behind. He was tall. I greeted him and asked him if he was Echosata and he said, "Indeed". I asked him to show me his sigil and he did. I introduced myself and he said, "Very well. Let's go for a walk". I quickly asked him, "By the way, what's this sandbox thing? I noticed symbols appearing in a pattern." He smiled and said, "Protection. But when people go near it, it will show a symbol which is related to them or associated with them. Let's see what yours is."

So we walked up and when I got close enough it again formed the triskele symbol. He asked, "Would you like to see more?" I said sure, but not knowing what he meant. We got closer to the sand and this time the triskele symbol rose up in the air, then slowly from the end of each spiral, the sand started to fall down and eventually completely disappeared. Then instantly a golden triskele formed. He nodded and said, "The Holy Trinity", then walked off. I asked him, "So is there a festival of some kind at this place? No disrespect, I was drenched and got covered in flower petals. I felt like I took a flower bath". He smiled and said, " In a way, it's a celebration. We get all kinds of guests here, so depending on who they are…" He did not finish his sentence, but I got the gist.

He turned around and said, "I want to show you my garden", and we came to the back of the house. It was huge. It wasn't just a garden, it was like another realm. I couldn't believe it. I asked him what he does there and he said everything. His work requires him to prepare for a lot of things and designs. He looked at me and said, "I see that you have these tattoos, does it work?" I said, "Only when I charge them." He said, "Well then, would you like something more permanent that doesn't require you to charge and that adapts to your needs?" I said, "Of course!" and in the air, he drew a symbol. I asked if he could draw it on me, so it could be active and start adapting, and he said, "Of course! More than delighted!" I showed him where and he drew it on me. It felt like a zap and a little burn, and it sunk in. Then he took me to a cave, it was round-shaped with a round hole up the top. I thought perhaps that is where the sunlight or the moonlight shines through. He said, "This is more like a place for meditation. You can get many revelations from here. Would you like to try?" I said, "Um, yeah sure, what do I have to do?" He said, "Just sit in the centre, don't fall asleep because I do sometimes, and try your best to remember all the details you see." Then he left.

I sat there at the centre looking at the blank walls. I noticed if I looked carefully that the walls weren't empty. There were layers of symbols, but none of which spoke to me. So I looked up and saw the sky. Suddenly, a white beam of light shot right through that hole into me. Then it vanished. I walked out and he asked, "What did you see?" I explained and he said, "Interesting" and he left it at that. Then we walked a little, came to a small bench and we sat down. In front of us was a small koi pond with a small waterfall. The water had shiny blue colour and the sky was the whole galaxy. There were lots of glowing bugs flying around making all sorts of colours. I told him, "I apologize, I am falling asleep, so perhaps don't tell me anything too important," He told me, "Then sleep." I then brought the rest of my legs onto the bench, curled, rested my head on his lap and closed my eyes. I got up leaving that body sleeping. He saw me do that. He too left his body sitting there with one hand on my head and came out. We were both in our light bodies. He said, "Very rarely people do that here, very well then." We were kind of hovering around and he was about to say something, but I found it hard to hear him. I felt how tired I was, and I apologized again. He smiled and said, "Go now and sleep. Rest well and I shall see you when you are awake." Then I got up.

Warning

Black magic can turn the **House of Protection and Wealth** into the **House of Failure.** According to the Picatrix and some other old grimoires, Azeruch wrath presides over: the destruction of merchandise, harvests and plants, putting discord between friends and between man and wife, debauching a woman you desire, and impeding those who journey so that they never reach the end of their road.

Negative influences from this Mansion may bring all kinds of failures: people may fail exams and job interviews, the journey may not pay off, trade may go wrong, plants may not grow and love may fail.

17ᵀᴴ Genius – Emzhom

Arabian Name: Adrieb
Western Tradition: Adriel
The Picatrix's Talisman: The figure of a monkey in an iron seal, holding his hands above his shoulders
Agrippa's Talisman: An ape
Bardon's Image: A man carrying a chest, followed by an ape
Emzhom is the head of the 17th Mansion: Alchil (Crown of Scorpio)
The Safe House: 25°42'52" Libra - 8°36'20" Scorpio
Position of the 17ᵗʰ Mansion in the Moon Zone: Astral part of the Moon. It is not easy to find it because it is somewhere below the Moon's waters. This region is similar to the one which is governed by Echotasa, but it is located on the completely opposite side of the Moon Zone.

Emzhom has the personality of an old, modest, patient, very wise and extremely observant angel. He often appears in different outfits. So, he can be seen with frizzy long hair, wearing ripped old clothes like a homeless person, but sometimes he appears wearing a grey robe with the hood up and covering most of his face and with his hands covered by his sleeves. He is also sometimes dressed "properly" with his hair nicely combed back. Emzhom is a very powerful head of the Moon Zone, which was also confirmed by Franz Bardon, "All moon beings look up to him in awe". Due to his extremely observant nature, he is not likely to teach magicians straight up what they seek. Instead, he will most likely closely observe and study the magician, and in the process, he will decide what is needed to be shown and taught. In his free time, he likes to play sports and board games.

Emzhom is similar to Emvatibe, the head of the 4th Lunar Mansion since both of them give banning formulae against malevolent spirits, people, energies and threatening situations. Emzhom works quite closely with the head of the Earth Zone Kiliosa (27° Capricorn), as both of them can reveal magical formulae which are essential for saving a magician's life in dire situations. Those formulae can paralyze any person or beast that is about to attack. Emzhom can also give magical formulae which can stop any negative Lunar influences, such as unsafe journeys, unhappy families, disunity, draught, dissatisfaction, etc. Those formulae are usually given under the seal of secrecy or are inherited. Franz Bardon has warned that they should be used only in case of real danger. This magician has also mentioned that Emzhom can teach banishing skills which can instantly destroy all enemies. So be warned to only use such formulae when it is absolutely necessary! And that goes without saying, that all can be possible only if the magician can successfully evoke Emzhom in such circumstances.

According to the Picatrix and other older magical scripts, one of Emzhom's main roles is to prevent thieves from entering into houses and to drive away criminals and all other people with negative intentions. Emzhom can teach the magician certain magical formulae that can instantly drive away or paralyze burglars, block their escape or make them return stolen goods. All in all, Emzhom is one of the best protectors of peoples' homes and properties.

Traditionally this genius assists with: creating strong foundations in the fields of building/construction, making strong and reliable relationships between people, long-lasting love, stable career, longevity, flourishing, and inspiring romance/passion that is fading. The last but not least, Emzhom can ground magicians anytime. In that regard, he can protect their legs to prevent injuries. If magicians tend to have any leg/ankle/feet-related issues, they can ask for his help. He will heal leg-related injuries quickly.

Emzhom has also an affinity with regard to water magic. He uses various unseen ways to teach the magician about water, but not as an element. Any advanced magician who seeks further knowledge in this area can ask for his wisdom. This genius is able to help you face your other half, the shadow aspect of yourself. He can also teach you how to use this particular skill any time you need.

Evocation Experiences

Talerman

My evocation of Emzhom did not last long, but he did teach me quite a lot. First of all, he gave me a proposal on how to conjure all the 28 Lunar angels by taking his own example:

Oh, great angel
at this moment
I am only standing at the gates
of the 17th Moon Mansion,
and of all what I am now seeing
there is nothing but the front door
of your Home.

I have some ideas about what might be inside
But my thoughts may be wrong,
so let me in,

*because I do not want to lie
to myself and others
about you and your great mysteries*

*So, I am ready to enter
And at this moment, that is actually
the only wish I have.*

*If you find me worthy,
please, open the gates
of the 17th Moon Mansion
so that I can enter in, see, learn,
and also touch on mysteries
hidden inside.*

*If you find me worthy,
please open the door.*

*I am not driven by you
by mere curiosity
but rather by the wish to learn
so that I would be more ready to assist.
As my capabilities grow,
the more I will be capable to help.*

*So, open the door for me
in the name of IHVH
Shaddai El Chai
and great Archangel Gabriel!*

*But if you do not find me worthy
Don't reject my honest and humble quest
for all eternity,
but let me improve what I need to improve
during the next month and let me try again in 28 days.*

During my evocation of Emzhop, it felt like it was raining heavily outside, but afterwards, I noticed that it had not. His sigil has obviously something to do with water and rain. Like many other Moon angels, he is clearly also a teacher of water. Interestingly, exactly as the previous head had done, he also invited me to play an interesting board game, which is well known on the Moon, but unheard of on the Earth.

KADILIYA

I found myself standing in the snow staring at my feet. Everything looked dim, but there was a triskele symbol hardly visible on the ground. Suddenly it rained, but the rain was blood, so the triskele got also filled with blood. On each of its spirals, there was a line which extended out reaching far away. On the left, it reached the forests, in the middle the urban cities, and on the right the ocean. Then there was a trail of blood leading to my feet. I looked at my hands and noticed that I was covered with blood too. I had the option to follow the lines to each location, but instead, I turned around. Then I saw an ice hole, so I decided to jump in. The water was freezing cold, but I kept swimming in the dark. I didn't know where I was going, but the entire time there was Emzhom's vibration in everything.

Suddenly an eye opened in front of me. I was a little scared but I faced the eye. It was golden and alive, but I didn't see the whole face. Then I swam up to the pupil and noticed I could walk in, so I did. At first, I thought I was falling but I was flying. After a long while, I saw a lake beneath me and I fell right in. After I surfaced, I looked around, and then realized that it was Echotasa's realm. I told myself that I needed to find Emzhom instead. So I swam in the opposite direction into nothingness. I was swimming until I noticed the water temperature change. It went cold very suddenly. As I dove down, I realized that the lake was connected to an ocean, so I kept swimming until another eye opened. This eye was silver-coloured. I swam right through its pupil and after that, I was sliding through a silver tunnel. During that time, I noticed a change in the vibration of the tunnel because it felt compacted. Very soon I was spat right through a waterfall. I swam up and looked around. There were lots of white flowers around and also a man sitting on a rock doing something. I walked out of the water, ringed out my hair and went up to the man.

He looked homeless and was fishing. I asked him, "Hello, are you Emzhom?" He looked at me and asked, "Do you like fishing?" I sat next to him on a rock and replied, "No, nor have I ever gone fishing". He asked, "What is it that you dislike about fishing?" I replied, "I think it's cruel. Even if people let the fish go. To a fish it is traumatizing, to the person it is exciting. I think it is cruel, especially when you are doing it as a sport". He quietly said, "Ah, a kind heart I see." I asked him if he liked fishing and he said, "Oh, I don't fish for fish. I like to see what comes out of that waterfall. Many interesting things come out from there sometimes." He got up and put away his fishing line which was, to my surprise, nothing more than a stick without the line or the hook. He started to walk into the dense jungle and I followed. I asked him again, "So, are you Emzhom?" He smiled and said that he was.

We came to a grassland. Far away there was a giant rock blocking an entrance to a cave. He said, "Do you recognize this place?" I replied "Yes". We went up to the rock and then he asked, "Tell me, do you have enemies?" I said "No." He said, "You must have because in your world everyone seems to have enemies." Then he turned around and I saw two people setting a nice table with two seats. There were lots of food displayed on the table. He gestured for me to sit, so I did, and he started to eat some pancakes. I noticed he no longer looked rugged but was dressed properly. I said, "Well, if you put it that way, then I do. I have only one enemy, and that is me," He asked, "Do you like pancakes? They are delicious, by the way, you should try some." I nicely declined and told him that I gotta avoid wheat, for now, so he told me to have some fruit then. "The berries are divine". Then there was a cup full of colourful but weirdly shaped berries in front of me. I got some on my spoon and put it in my mouth (let's just say that inside my mouth there was a party). He swallowed his last bite of the pancake and wiped his mouth clean. He asked if I would like to try some divinely delicious tea and I agreed.

He continued, "So your enemy is yourself? Then, would you like to know how to defeat that enemy?" I replied, "Well, I don't want to defeat my enemy because that itself carries a negative connotation. I want to be able to face my enemy and see it as who it truly is." He gestured, "Continue…" I said, "I want to be brave and not run away. I am tired of running away. I am tired of not being able to see the truth. Each chance I get I run away from myself and I'm growing very tired of that. I've faced many things in my life. Whatever that was thrown at me I faced it one way or another, but when it comes to myself, I'm completely helpless." He nodded and said, "Good, when you see this, what do you feel?" And all of a sudden, I saw myself facing a huge tall wave which was about to hit hard. I couldn't talk. I was stuck at that moment, but when I realized that, I stood up and faced the wave. Still, I felt scared. I turned around. There were lots of people and their homes behind me. I felt worried for them. Then Emzhom walked up to me and quietly said, "You have a lot of water, and it has a very destructive side to it. I can see the horror in your eyes. I can feel your pain and your fear. First tell me, what causes big waves?" I replied with a shaky voice, "There is wind, gravity…I don't know". He said, "So there is the element of wind. What is wind associated with?" I replied quickly, "The mental, thoughts…" And he said, "Yes, the mental. When you face a situation with all kinds of thoughts, what happens after that?" I replied, "You react. Your first response is a reaction." I was still facing this tall disastrous wave. He asked, "But if you go deep and push away the thoughts and the reactions, what do you feel?" I said, "Sadness." I do not know why, but at that point, I felt relief. He continued, "Yes, sadness, behind all reactions there are emotions."

I suddenly realized the waves were just a reaction to my emotions. I decided to walk towards them and I felt there was someone standing behind them. I walked and parted the waves when I saw a young teenager. She was so mad, her eyes spoke rage, and her aura was destructive, but beneath all, I felt something else about her. I went to her to calm her down, but my voice soon changed to Emzhom's voice which was saying, "The physical world is harmonious, but only thanks to some people who bring harmony. Most people go through day-to-day, battling within themselves to survive. All people have their own inner conflicts and they don't know what to do, so they react. Everyone also feels alone, no matter the situation. When that distortion comes to play, it is time to quieten down the mind, reflect and wait. Somewhere within all creation, there is that faint sound of love. Immerse in it, be it, become it. It might be temporary, but you must remind yourself of that love every time when there is conflict. Humans get hurt easily but also recover miraculously. Beneath all that pain there is love. Just like the waves of your oceans or stormy skies, once they are gone, there will be stillness, beauty and light. Learn the flow of your surroundings, learn the flow of your adaptations and reconfigure what does not serve. Evolve!"

Warning

Black magic can turn the **Safe House** into the **House of Destruction and Confusion.**

Magicians may get tempted to use Emzhom's magical formulae against innocent people, if for nothing else, then for mere curiosity's sake to check whether they work or not. Since banning formulae are usually given to the magician under the seal of secrecy, if anyone gets tempted to disclose them unauthorized, they will likely lose their powers at once, so they will not work when it is needed. As for another side-effect of working with this angel, the magician might get confused and forget which formulae to use while under a sudden attack.

No magicians should ever take Emzhom's teachings so lightly and carelessly. Especially his magical formulae to affect certain events or people should be left alone if there is no real reason to use them. Not only can they backfire bringing bad luck to magicians who used them carelessly, but they can also make them seriously ill (either around the brain region or the bottom half of the body).

18ᵀᴴ Genius – Emzhit

Arabian Name: Egibiel
Western Tradition: Egribel
Picatrix's Talisman: The image in wax of an adder holding its tail above its head
Agrippa's Talisman: A snake holding its tail above its head
Bruno's Image: A man with a golden snake in his hand, which many serpents flee from
Emzhit is the Head of the 18th Mansion: Alchas ili Altob (Heart of Scorpio)
House of Healing and Manifestations: 08°36'2" - 21°25'44" Scorpio
Position of the 18th Mansion in the Moon Zone: Tree of Life of Yesod

Emzhit appears as a middle-aged black-haired noble male spirit dressed in black with bright golden reflective eyes which he uses for healing and making other wonders. He is very close to Archangel Gabriel. He was traditionally asked to help against fever and stomachache, but he can heal other illnesses as well. Emzhit ensures that medicine will work efficiently. He is considered to be one of the best healers from the Moon. According to some old mystical tradition, Emzhit teaches the magician how to control and tame snakes and wild beasts, and also how to protect from all snake-related injuries.

Franz Bardon revealed other Emzhit's faculties which focus on materialization, dematerialization, manifestations, phenomenal magic and invisibility. In this regard, Emzhit is similar to Ebvep, the head of the 11th Mansion, and also to a few related heads of the Earth Zone such as Agasoly, Nimtrix, Masadu, Pagalusta and Camalo.

Emzhit is one of the most important guardians of Lunar gates, which gives him the power to control all kinds of materialization and manifestations. Certain things from the astral plane will never materialize in the physical reality due to their resistance towards the matter or for some karmic reasons. If that is not the case, and most often it is not, Emzhit or his subordinate spirits will help with materialization. They can teach the magician how to transform or transmute 9 to 10.

On a very advanced level, Emzhit instructs the magician how to become invisible in all three spheres. That being said, Emzhit and his subordinate spirits have saved many non-initiated people by making them invisible to their enemies.

Emzhit is one of the best experts on the Tree of Life from the Moon Zone. Each sephira has its own inner Tree of Life, so if you want to learn more about the Tree of Life of Yesod, ask Emzhit for help. This spirit might be one of the most important guardians of the Tree of Life of Yesod. Emzhit is also closely related to ancient Nordic mysteries. Like some other genii of the Moon, he likes social games.

Evocation Experiences

Talerman

I was thinking about Kadiliya during this evocation because she told me that she was ill. At one moment I saw Emzhit lifting Isis in his arms and hugging her. After that, I complained to Emzhit about my own headache. At the same moment I saw him watching me with his bright eyes, and out of them came out the lasers straight into my head. The procedure was not finished because it was very loud outside as some workers were rebuilding the pavement. Nevertheless, the headache was gone.

I also noticed some other spirits in my house with whom I had started working quite recently, so I took this chance to greet them too. They were busy playing with my crystals and cleaning my altar. Emzhit showed me a new board game which is popular on the Moon, books for children about animals, and funny comics about ducks. It is obvious that Lunar spirits adore children.

KADILIYA

My first attempt on Emzhit failed. It might be that my energy level was pretty low. Throughout the night I had dreams of war between different racial groups. It got very bloody and cruel, so I woke up feeling even more tired.

During the writing of this book, before I went to bed, I thought of Emzhit and why I had not had success with this spirit, so I called Gabriel to help me connect with Emzhit once more. Very quickly I felt very light, so I left my bedroom and went somewhere. The very first thing I saw was slow-motion golden sand pouring from somewhere to something. Then everything was dark. I could not see anything. I could only hear banging or clanking noise from two ends like someone was making something. An image of the golden sand appeared to be poured into hot lava. The lava travelled through the crevices of some metal which formed out of it a shape of a long rod. I looked up and realized I was inside some blacksmith shop. There were silver spirits making golden long rods. Once made, they would pass rods to others and they would take them up into the clouds. I followed them up where I could see that there were no clouds, but a certain element in the sky that looked like clouds. There were all kinds of shops (or structures like shops) all over this place and silver beings were just hovering from one place to another. They could walk up, sideways or curved. In the background, there was a sound of bells chiming softly and brightly, but I couldn't pinpoint where it was coming from. I asked one of the spirits where they were taking the rods and they replied "Emzhit, the Holy." And I asked, "For what purpose?" And they replied "Structures for the Holy of the Holy," and then they left.

I heard a faint voice that said, "If you so choose, you may follow." And that was Gabriel. I went with the spirits and came to this place where there were millions of these spirits putting these golden rods onto something that resembled bridges. There were so many bridges I lost count. I noticed these rods weren't solid. They were made of energy. When I looked closely, I noticed something was moving within these things. I looked even closer and saw energy particles travelling through a rod and I could hear voices. I put my ear against it and heard so many different kinds of communication. Some sounded so familiar, so I focused on a few particulars and I heard conversations being held between some Lunar spirits and other magicians and between Lunar spirits and some spirits from Tipharet. I got very curious. I stood back and noticed a particular flower growing at the bottom of these bridges. But I brought my focus back on Emzhit. Still nothing. I looked at the bridges once more to see where they went. Something looked peculiar which was that they all lead somewhere up and down. I followed them down and to my surprise, they were connected to another big spirit. The spirit looked like a female. I say the spirit because it had a layout of a female figure with long hair, which instantly reminded me of a painting I had done two years ago.

All of a sudden two golden reflective eyes appeared with a face of an old man with high cheekbones and sunken eyes wearing a long robe with a hood. His hands were clasped at his sternum. I asked, "Are you Emzhit?" And he said he was. I asked for his sigil and he confirmed it was by using the names of the Holy ones. His movements were rapid but in slow motion. His energy was moving at an extreme rate yet slowly. I asked him, "What is this bridge?" He replied, "These are not bridges, these are the roots of a tree." I asked "What tree?" He replied "Tree of Yesod." I continued with my questions and asked, "Where do they go? Why do they connect to this spirit at the bottom? What is the purpose?" And he said, "They go to the rest of the Tree of Life. They connect to this spirit because this spirit is linked to the Tree of Life. This connection is the very reason why this spirit can travel throughout Yesod as it pleases. The purpose is to inform." I asked, "Why is it called Holy?" He said, "It is holy because it is the connection to the subconscious and to the unconscious. Is it not an act of the Holy when one reaches for the Divine? To become one with the infinite?" I further asked, "Why couldn't I find you or reach you in the past?" He said, "Time was not ready. Negative aspects of Yesod were heavy, planets were not aligned accordingly." I asked, "So now they are?" And he said, "Yes, but more importantly The Will is mature." Again I asked, "What is the purpose of this experience?" He replied, "Revelation."

    I gained his sigil and permission to record this. This spirit spoke in the ancient tongue of Norse. I kept hearing Jötunheimr and its connection to Yesod. I do not know why, but I also kept getting the name Mimir. It was revealed to me that Mimir is one of Emzhit's subordinate spirits. Both have golden reflective eyes. And another manifestation of Mimir is a golden-eyed snake.

Warning

Black magic can turn the House of **Health and Manifestations** into the **House of Illnesses and Evil Creations.**

According to the Picatrix, Egrebel wrath is useful for: men to conspire against kings, vengeance against enemies and whatever else of the nature of vengeance, conspiracy, and separate friends.

Immature magicians might be tempted to abuse Emzhit's knowledge to create something that is evil of nature or even spread illnesses. Alternatively, they may also try to prevent other people from healing or from manifestations of what they desire. Those people who use black magic with the help of the negative influence of this Lunar spirit can bring drought, barren lands, sickness, or prevent healing even when all the necessary elements for healing are present. If the magician comes across anything of that nature, they are strongly advised to call Emzhit at once for his help in the name of Archangel Gabriel and Shaddai El Chai.

19th Genius – Emzheme

Arabian Name: Annucel
Western Tradition: Amutiel
The Picatrix's Talisman: The image of a woman holding her hands in front of her face
Agrippa's Talisman: A woman holding her hands upon her face
Bruno's Image: A woman in childbirth with her hands over her face
Emzheme is the head of the 19 Mansion: Allatha or Achala (Scorpio's Tail)
House of the Moon and the Earth: 21°25'44" Scorpio - 4°27'44" Sagittarius
Position of the 19th Mansion in the Moon Zone: Not specified. Some parts of his region are on the Moon but also on the Earth and everything in between. This genius is also famous for creating his own realms too

Emzheme is a great divine angel. He is very helpful. This genius is especially keen on helping out any initiates who are struggling in life or with their magical practices. This angel is not quite like other Lunar spirits in terms of his teaching style. He can be seen as a spirit that creates realms for different purposes and sometimes in accordance with his student's needs. Emzheme is one of the best initiators of the Moon Zone. He is also very closely related to the Earth. Most of his time he spends on our planet. Once the contact has been established, the magician may communicate with this angel easily through prayers.

This angel always suggests we spend more time in nature. Apart from all things he teaches about the Earth and the Moon and in between, this angel also brings peace, the release of war prisoners, safety to refugees, peaceful journeys on the sea and good luck to sailors. Emzheme's talismans were traditionally used for facilitating birth and against menstrual problems.

One of his faculties focuses on all connections between the Moon and the Earth. In this respect, he is similar to the following heads from the Earth Zone whose faculty is an analogy: Golemi (10° Gemini), Kaflesi (28° Gemini), Sibolas (29° Gemini), Nelion (29° Aquarius), and Elipinon (23° Virgo).

Emzheme teaches the magician to evaluate different beings from the Moon sphere. He gives instructions on how to make analogies between the Moon on one side and the Earth, spirits, nature, people, body parts, stones, plants and animals on the other. Emzheme also teaches about the Moon in symbols, tarot, Yi-Jing, runes, alchemy, chiromancy and astrology. He is considered to be one of the best experts on etheric connections between the Earth and the Moon, the Moon's rays, cycles, rhythms, circulations and phases. Emzheme is excellent at interpreting the deepest meaning of the Moon tarot card.

Additional Observations Relevant to Emzheme's Teachings

Silver

It facilitates connections to the Moon's energies. Alchemists call it the "metal of Luna" or the "metal of Diana" and symbolize it with a half-moon crescent. Old Egyptians thought that their god Ra had silver bones. They used silver in their magical rituals and their rings and scarab figures were often silvery. The Incas compared silver to "the tears of the Moon". Western "Milky Way" is the Chinese "Silver River". Many magicians and witches prefer silver to any other metal. Silver has a good protective power against negative forces for which reason it has been frequently used for amulets too. Many stories about silver and its use in magic are yet to be told to people by Emzheme and some other similar spirits.

Colours of the Moon

Emzheme may instruct which colour to use when evoking Lunar spirits. William Lilly connects in his book "Christian Astrology", 1647, the Moon with white, yellowish-white, pale green and silvery colours. Franz Bardon has said that Lunar spirits appear in their silvery lights and that the magician has to create white light during the evocation. Bardon has further suggested sigils to be drawn in silver or white colours for the first evocations of the genii from the Moon. Eliphas Levi used to wear white clothes decorated with silver silk and silver letters when he evoked spirits from the Moon. Yesod is also often presented in purple colour and the magician may also use that colour if he wants to connect to lunar energies.

Lunar Stones

Emzheme teaches the magician how to use moonstones, pearls, crystal quartzes, beryls, and many other whites, green and soft stones for divination, amulets, protection against epilepsy and madness, agricultural growth, safe travels, shamanistic rituals, lucid dreams and against storms and drownings.

Lunar Oils and Plants

The following oils are connected to the Moon: lavender, camphor, amber, white sandalwood, jasmine, ylang-ylang, Iris root and eucalyptus. Aleister Crowley connects all opiate perfumes to the Moon. For William Lilly, the Lunar vegetables are cabbage, lentil, beans, cucumber, pumpkin, gourd and carrot. Lunar flowers are rosemary (according to Agrippa), poppy (according to Lilly) and jasmine (according to Crowley). Other Lunar flowers are angel trumpet, narcissus, lily and iris. Other Lunar associates are mushrooms, mandrake, orchids' root, egg white, fat (in the Islam culture, when praying over cooking fat, the prayers are delivered to the deceased ancestors via the smell/fumes of fat) and aloha. The Lunar trees are Willow, Linden, Olive and Coco. According to William Lilly, the Lunar are all trees with round, dark and wide leaves. Emzheme can share a lot of untold stories about this subject with the magician.

Lunar Animals

Old Egyptians venerated cats as their sacred lunar animals. Ever since that time cats have been the favourite pets of many magicians and witches. In more modern times, hermetists associated elephants with Yesod. Agrippa says that Lunar animals are: dogs, cats, baboons, panthers, lynxes, mice, and all water animals. According to William Lilly, Lunar animals are frogs, otters, geese, ducks, owls, sea birds, cuckoos, shells, fish, crabs, and turtles. Traditionally Lunar animals are also: the ox, winded ox, pig, crow, hyena, hydra, rabbit and Minotaur.

The Moon and the Human Body

In physiognomy, there are Solar, Lunar, Saturnine, Mercurial, Venusian, Jovial, Martial and Mundane types of people. Emzheme teaches the magician about analogies between the Moon and the human body. The Lunar face is wide, round and pale; small or middle in seizing and sometimes not confident. The forehead is wide, the nose short, the hair light-brown and the eyes grey or watery. Moon Hill is one of the most important characteristics of the human palm. Occult talents are recognized by the triangle on Moon Hill. A person is about to travel frequently if his palm's lines lead towards his or her Moon Hill. If your Moon Hill is large, your spiritual potentials are also good.

EVOCATION EXPERIENCES

TALERMAN

During my evocation of Emzheme, I saw many spirits and was also involved in different seemingly unrelated situations which were all somehow supervised by this head. I saw an American military officer giving a speech about magic to a large audience, and for some reason, his knowledge of magic was very much appreciated by all. However, I noticed something suspicious about him and his speech. I came up to him and interrupted his lecture, while others were watching me surprisingly. I said, "This man is not here." A few people from the audience said: "How do you know that?" I told them to look more carefully at the chair where he was supposedly sitting and said again: "This man is not here!" I don't know how I knew it, but I did it anyway and was right about it. After a while, all agreed that that person was definitely not there.

Later the same group audience was watching a movie about Ivo Andric, the Nobel prize winner in literature from my country. Some of them said that Ivo Andric had become a very honoured magician after his death, and for this reason, they had read carefully all of his books. I did not watch the whole movie with them, but I did observe a few mistakes in it, so I told them what they were about. How did I know that and what mistakes did I find in the move? I don't know. Nevertheless, they listened to my remarks carefully and thanked me

After that, I was somewhere else. I walked on an empty road in a village. There was only one woman, not much different from women in our world's reality. I asked her what the name of this region was. She said that was the Earth. I asked this lady, "Can you be more specific?" And she said, "This is the Earth of Earth." I thanked her very much. This was actually for me the first time to ever hear any spirit talking about regions of Malkuth using the hermetic terminology about elements such as Earth of Earth, Water of Earth, Fire of Earth, Air of Earth, etc. I found it very interesting, but I realized that I had not yet seen Emzheme. So I continued my search for him which lasted more or less all night long. In the meantime, I continued to have interesting conversations with a few of my new spiritual friends whom I met earlier that day.

Finally, somewhere by the end of this very long magical session, I saw how my altar in the room was becoming incredibly sacred, really Divine. A few new statues of divinities which were somehow obviously alive were appearing on it. One of them was a statue of Emzheme. I found this angel truly Divine and maybe for this reason I had great very difficulty meeting him.

KADILIYA

My quest started with me standing before a green hill with a white flag on the top. I got closer - the flag was just plain white, but over the hill, there was a black hole swirling. A man appeared from behind. He was wearing a mask. I asked if he was Emzheme and he said he was while removing his mask. I asked him, "What was down there?" And he said, "Dense energy whirlpool, where the lost souls tend to gather." I asked if they can be helped and he said, "Yes, but that's not why you've come here." He said, "So you didn't find Emzhit?...Well, maybe next time."

At this point, we lay on the grass staring at the sky. He asked me what was wrong and I replied, "I'm having an inner conflict, whether to believe in any of this or not. As to believe in you, could you just be part of my imagination? It's not real". He said, "I can see the negative aspect of the Lunar is affecting you. You are battling your biggest problem which is your confidence. Why?" I replied "I'm afraid that none of this is real, and if it is, I'm merely just a vessel. The spirits are working through me and that's all." He said, "Take my hand, I want to take you to a place." I did and so we entered a white space. Everything was white but I could see some things. I asked, "Where are we?" He said, "Here, it's my creation. I created this place for this purpose. How do you feel now?" I said, "Little lighter", and he replied, "Perhaps a little better too? Ah yes. We are away from the dense place, your emotions were magnifying."

Then I saw a spring and we both went in and sat in. We conversed for a while regarding the matter of my worries. Unfortunately, though, I let it succumb to me so I left. After an hour I decided to go back in again. It began with us being in the spring together. He said, "You're back!" I replied "Yes! Now, tell me what do I have to do?" He got up and asked me to go to a place with him and he took me to a garden. There were lots of little flowers, from dark blue to light blue, almost like the spectrum of blues. I felt warm and happy. He said, "The flowers don't have mirrors to see what they look like. Each flower speaks to one another and it's in the language of love. You don't ever see them fighting over vanity, or feeling jealous of each other, nor do you ever hear them talk about anything of such nature. They rely on each other, they blossom from within, and they connect heart to heart. They know their true beauty, they are at their best. Why judge, why worry? They are part of the creation. They are blooming within the Creator's Will,' I sighed. He continued, "Go deep, deep into your heart, go into your heart space and feel it. What does it feel like?"

I went deep. I saw my heart's space and I felt this vibration that cannot be denied. I replied, "It feels real, I am real. It feels authentic. Almost as if nothing else matters, only this, the heart matters." He smiled and said, "Everything else is on the surface and that creates unstable thought forms leading you to all kinds of places." He said, "Don't let certain information you learn about yourself cloud your mind. It's good to know and expand knowledge regarding the 'self'. In fact, it's crucial. But often people stop there, content with what they think they know and go about their days with that in mind. That state of mind often leads one to delusional thoughts, distorted thoughts and even entitlement. Distorted thought forms give birth to chaos. The universe is ever-growing, remember that. Should you learn something new, check in with the heart and see if that resonates." All that sat heavily with me but not in a bad way. Lots to contemplate.

Warning

Black magic can turn the **House of the Moon and the Earth** into the **House of Destruction.** According to the Picatrix, Annucel wrath is used to: besiege cities and villages and claim them, destroy the wealth of whomever you please, expel men from a particular place, break and destroy ships, separate and destroy the riches of allies, and kill captives.

20ᵀᴴ Genius – Etsacheye

Arabian Name: Kvejhuk
Western Tradition: Kyriel
The Picatrix's Talisman: A figure having the head and arms of a man, the body of a horse with four feet and a tail, holding a bow in its hands
Agrippa's Talisman: Sagittarius, half man and half horse.
Bruno's Talisman: A hunting centaur, with a quiver on his back and a bow in his left hand, with a dead fox in his right hand
Etsacheye is the head of the 20th Mansion: Abnahaya (Sagittarius)
House of Hunting, Animals and Ecstasy: 04°27'10" 17°8'26" Sagittarius
Position of the 20ᵗʰ Mansion in the Moon Zone: Not specific. Abundant nature with lots of animals and plants, wherever it may be on the Moon Zone, belongs at least partly to his region

Etsacheye is a male spirit that is seen dressed casually. He is rarely alone and often surrounded by many spirits, animals and creatures, like centaurs and unicorns around him of whom some might even look familiar to the magician for some usually unknown reasons. This genius is lighthearted and very outgoing in personality.

One of Etsacheye's faculties teaches about the understanding of animals. When the Moon was in his Mansion traditionally back in the old days, people were suggested to spend time with domestic animals, hunt and or buy animals.

This spirit is a protector of hunters (like Petuno from the Earth Zone), and as such he is also closely related to Diana and other gods and goddesses associated with hunting. If magicians do not want to hunt animals, Etsacheye can help them get or catch whatever else they want (job, love, money, good school, good medicine, etc). His arrows do not miss. Neither will you miss, if he was sent to you as a guardian.

Etsacheye's influence is to encourage people to explore and dig deeper into their animalistic nature, essentially to embrace themselves to the fullest. He was behind many ecstatic witch ceremonies. He can tell many forgotten or untold stories about ancient bacchanalias. This spirit is very close to: Pan, Dionysus, Daphnis, Priapus, Silenus, Hermaphrodites, Kefallos, etc. Those gods and semi-gods of nature adore nature, entertainment, wine, women, fairies and music. Etsacheye is one of those spirits who will always encourage people to break free from their busy schedules so that they can live and enjoy life.

Etsacheye is a special guardian of all those dervish dancers and other mystical dancers. He is the master of occult dancing and he is similar to Kolani (20° Gemini), the head of the Earth Zone. Etsacheye's subordinate spirits have been present wherever and whenever dancing has been involved to achieve mystical visions and ecstasy. Many Jewish occult dancers, Dervish masters, Christian mystics and Latin American shamans join Etsacheye or Kolani when they die.

Franz Bardon pointed out that Etsacheye teaches the magician how to gain supremacy over positive as well as negative spirits of the Moon. In this regard, Etsacheye may teach magicians to focus on the highest aspects and powers of the Moon, as they would in return help them gain such supremacy.

In the cabalistic tradition, the mightiest powers related to the Moon are YHVH, Shaddai El Chai and Archangel Gabriel.

To magicians who want to gain supremacy over all Lunar spirits, but worship Greek-Roman ancient cults, the main assistant in this regard is Diana (Artemis). She shares her love for hunting, wildlife and ecstasy with Etsacheye. Other magicians may gain supremacy over all Lunar spirits if they worship mighty Lunar gods or goddesses from other traditions, such as Alako, Nanna, Chandra, Marama, Chang E, etc. You may always ask Etsacheye for suggestions if you are not sure what gods or goddesses are from the Moon to the warship.

Additional Observations Relevant to Etsacheye's Teachings

Diana

She has many names: The One who gives Life, Wanderer in the Wilderness, Virgin Hunter, The One with the Silver Bow, Arrow of Light, The Healer, Diana of the Hills, Lady of Magic Spells, Lady of Dancing, Protector of Travellers, Protector of Virgins, The One who shines, and Protector of Wild Beast. When she was very young, she strove for independence and adventures, so she asked Zeus to give her a bow and an arrow and to let her run in the wilderness together with her nymphs and dogs. Consequently, she became a protector of forests, wilderness, wild beasts and virgins. The old Greeks depicted her sometimes with wings, similar to how the Christians see angels. Diana is keen on heroes and it's not possible to evoke her unless the magician had done a heroic deed in her honour. If the magician is more connected to Hecate or Selena, call them instead for help to gain supremacy over all lunar spirits.

Hecate

Hippolytus writes the following conjuration to Hecate in his work "Philosophumena" from the 3rd Century: "Come, you, hellish, earthly and heavenly Hecate, the goddess of wide roads and crossroads, who wanders at night with a torch in your hand. You, the enemy of the day and the friend of lovers' nights, you who enjoys when the wolves howl, who walks around the graves...have a look at our offering."

Selena

In the Homeric hymns, she appears as a wonderful goddess with a silver colour, long wings, and a golden diadem as decoration on her head. She was worshipped by Greeks during the Full Moon, but they did not build temples in her honour.

Other Lunar Gods and Goddesses:

- Alako or Dungra, a protector of Gypsies and their guide in the afterlife, is probably the only Lunar god who was continuously worshipped in Europe until the 19th century.
- Nanna, Lord of destiny and wisdom from Ur.
- Chandra, the Indian god of the Moon, has white colour and white decorations and drives a white chariot pulled by ten white horses or ten antelopes.
- Tsukiomi, the Japanese god of the Moon.
- Yue Lao, the Chinese god of marriage, stays on the Moon from where he connects people destined to marry with his red yarn.
- Chang E, the Chinese Moon goddess, holds the lunar disk in her hand

- Amogapaka, the Buddhist deity, has white colour, eight arms and stands on the Moon from where he is catching just people with his lasso.
- Akokakanta, the Buddhist female deity, has golden-yellow colour, is dressed in white, rides a pig or stands on the Moon above a lotus.
- Wang Shu and Kisan A - the two Taoist genii of the Moon, recognized by the master Huainan Ziyu.
- Hini, a witch from the Polynesian Island, became a goddess and now lives on the Moon.
- Marama is the Maori goddess of the Moon worshipped in New Zealand. Her body occasionally disappears but appears again in its full beauty when she takes a bath in the water of life.

EVOCATION EXPERIENCES

TALERMAN

I saw Etsacheye's etheric shape in my room, but I did not receive any clear message from him, except for the vision of a fox, dog, and a wolf. Were they there by chance or were they Etsacheye's subordinate spirits, I was not able to understand, so, I closed my ritual, but later on I continued to search for his signs in my everyday life activities. At one moment, in the evening, when I was in the city square heading for the metro station, I looked up at the sky and saw the Moon, so I greeted it in the name of IHVH, Shaddai El Chai and Etsacheye, and the Moon came much closer to me. Then I saw hundreds of people walking around not paying attention to each other, and yet they all were interconnected by delicate silver links. Besides, each person was also connected to the Moon. Suddenly, I saw millions of fine silver tracks connecting the Earth with the Moon. I felt shamanic and that we all are one. I greeted Etsacheye, bowed to the Moon, and hurried up to catch the train. Later that night, I saw I few very beautiful fairy spirits with light green and brown eyes. They told me that they had been sent by Etsacheye to greet me.

KADILIYA

It began with me slowing down my breathing. I was using my breath to send out Qi which carried Etsacheye's name. Soon my breath colour changed. It was blue-silver filling up the air around me. Suddenly I was inside a bubble that was silver and blue and it started moving. I came to a place where everything was filled with tiny sparkles of blue. I looked around. I saw something move far away, so I went to investigate. I came to something I had not been able to see before. It was a female-shaped body made out of millions of blue sparkles. I instantly recognized her. I had this strong familiar feeling that I knew her and I knew it was not Etsacheye, but the gatekeeper instead.

She came up to me and we were very happy to see each other. She said, "It's been a while since I last saw you! You're looking well!" Then we danced around like two mermaids swimming in the galaxy. Something started forming behind us. I looked briefly and it looked like a seal. I was so happy to see my friend, so we kept dancing and laughing until a circular thing opened. I thanked her and walked in. Everything turned golden, the air was soft and smelled beautiful. Again that feeling rose inside me as if I had been here before. I saw a man wearing slippers and shorts, sunnies and thick hair. He was watering plants. I went up closer and I could hear the plants singing, and see some interesting creatures lurking around.

He turned and said, "Oh! Haven't I seen you before? Heh, I'm just joking. Nice to see you back here again". I asked if he was Etsacheye even though I knew it was him, and he confirmed. I apologized and said, "I know I've been here before, but I can't seem to put the pieces together". He smiled and said. "I see, all in good time. So why are you here again?' I replied, "Well, I'm visiting the 28 Lunar Mansions which seem to be leading me to learn more about myself than anything. I've come to check you and your realm out. But it seems so familiar...Is there anything you could show me or perhaps teach me?"

He jumped and floated in the air like laying down staring at the skies and said, "Well, you already know what you need to know. You just gotta dig deeper. Go deep into your soul, into your light and you'll find what you are looking for. It's all in there tucked away. Go deep. You can definitely do it. You still remembered how to open the gates, didn't you? Just like that, don't hesitate". Then he gave me a big smile and sent me off.

Warning

Black magic can turn the **House of Hunting, Animals and Ecstasy** into the **House of Self Destruction.**

The black magician can be tempted to experiment with the retrograde Moon in order to push other people to dance or perform other ecstatic practices, such as bacchanalian-like orgies, till they would seriously harm themselves or even die. Immature magicians and other spiritual seekers may be drawn by such ecstatic and orgiastic practices even to suicide. Such tragic events among them are luckily very rare, but what often happens is that they use magic as a pretext for their profanities.

On the other side, many Wiccans and other Moon worshippers are led to see themselves as successors of old traditions and some of their branches are said to follow cults of old Thessalonian witches who used to be able to control the Moon. Yet, much of what modern Wicca does now is the fruit of its own inventions or misinterpretations of the ancient sources. Such rituals might be fun, but it is a question of how much they can also be spiritually and magically beneficial. If the magician encounters some modern cults and sects that worship the Moon, but are in doubt about their rituals and intentions, ask Etsacheye for help and he will reveal whether they are genuine or not!

21ˢᵗ Genius – Etamrezh

Arabian Name: Bectue
Western Tradition: Bethnael
Etamrezh is the head of the 21ˢᵗ Mansion: Abeda or Albedach
The House of Mastery of Life and Death: 17°08'48" Sagittarius - 0°0'0 Capricorn
Position of the 20ᵗʰ Mansion in the Moon Zone: Not specific. Hardly approachable
Talismans and Images: Traditionally used for malevolent purposes, they are presented in the 'Warning' section of this entry

Etamrazh is a male spirit that is seen dressed neatly. His face is not very clear. He is strongly built and can also be seen sometimes with a mighty beard. This genius happens to mostly teach angels and other advanced spirits from the Earth, the Moon and other planets. He teaches them: advanced elemental magic, advanced mummial magic and other forms of magic that cannot be named. Magicians who evoke him might not be able to work with or alongside him immediately in the beginning due to the nature of his advanced faculties. And especially, which is in most cases, if the magician is not ready, Etamrezh will tell them to come back at a later time.

He is one of the greatest masters of the mummial magic, in which he is similar to Emcheba, the head of the 13ᵗʰ Mansion.

The main difference between them two in the mummial magic is that Etamrezh's instructions are focused on invulnerability, while Emcheba's are on longevity. Franz Bardon mentions that with Etamrezh's help the magician will "become strong and resistant against any visible and invisible enemies, against any kind of influence by elements, etc". And, the magician will become "a magical taboo" and "invulnerable from the magical point of view and master over his life and death."

Etamrezh is also one of the greatest experts on the fire element from the Moon Zone. In this regard, he is similar to Tabbata (10° Leo), a head and a high priest of fire from the Earth Zone, whose faculty is also invulnerable, especially when it is against the element of fire. Etamrezh can make magicians capable of enduring the greatest possible heat and may teach them how to worship fire, and even how to play and kiss with its spirits. When it comes to the other elements, he can instruct the magician how to survive the most extreme weather conditions caused by the water and earth elements.

Etamrezh is one of the most active spirits from the Moon Zone. This mighty genius can give one a lot of opportunities to practice sports. Especially in martial arts, ask Etamrezh for help.

Traditionally, he was asked for help to increase harvests, make a profit, save money, and go safely through the countryside. When the Moon was in its 21st Mansion, it was an excellent time to start a new enterprise.

Etamrezh is also one of the best guardians of witches. He empowers them, passes to their knowledge and protection, and helps them in love matters. On the other hand, if you have a problem with witches, ask them for help! If you want to meet a witch, he will make it happen via different connections. This spirit can teach magicians how to protect themselves from any magical attack, devastation and destruction. He is especially good at protecting people if they are magically attacked by women. If a woman cast a curse, hex, or spell on an individual, ask Etamrezh for help! When the Moon is in this Mansion, pay attention not to irritate women in the next 24 hours. This genius will encourage everyone to improve relations with their wives and women in general.

Evocation Experiences

Talerman

My first evocation of Etamrezh was quick. He appeared first in my triangle as an etheric figure, and then in my OBE as a powerful and strong bearded man. I asked him if he was willing to teach me about mysteries within his Mansion, but I could not catch if he said anything. But what I did clearly see was his index finger pointed at me. I hope it meant that he chose me, but I don't know for sure.

Later he said that I was still not ready for his advanced teaching, so he changed the subject talking about sports, hobbies and other lighter topics. He said that Lunar people like all kinds of sports. While he was talking about it, I saw some spirits play with gravitation, move fast, bi-locate and teleport with utter easiness. I saw a football stadium that was occupied to the last seat. I heard again Etamrezh's voice. He said that they on the Moon have all sports we have on Earth, but that they additionally also practice some sports disciplines that we do not have. And then I was back to this world's reality.

Kadiliya

The vision started with lightning flashing throughout the sky. Everything seemed dark. One lightning bolt hit a tree, so I went to check it. The tree was burnt to ashes. I looked up and saw a visible opening in the sky, so I jumped through. I seemed to be travelling through many places very fast until I was able to stand somewhere. I looked up and there was a giant burning lion beast standing in front of a palace. He asked me, "What is your business here?" I replied that I was visiting all the Lunar Mansions and that this happened to be on the list. He asked me again, "And what have you learned so far?" I replied that mostly about myself. He paused briefly and said, "Very well, you may pass". Then the gate opened and he was gone. Before I went in I noticed the opening of the gate had a circular seal that resembled that beast.

I walked in and it was dark until a small light appeared. I followed that light until the bottom of my feet started to glow. I looked down and I saw a disk light up. It had interesting designs all over it. Then more disks lit up. I could suddenly feel a presence, but I couldn't see it. I asked, "Are you Etamrezh?", and a voice came through that said, "Yes, I am". A foot, steps through the light, and then from the legs and up, a person appeared. He was wearing a dress, shoes, black jeans, a black shirt and a golden medallion. His face was, however, light, so I couldn't see it. I was just about to introduce myself, but he interrupted and said, "I know who you are, and why you've come. However, you're not ready for the knowledge I can give. At least, not yet. After you have finished visiting everyone else, come back to me, and I will have something for you. You may leave now". Then I was all the way back at the gate and I came out. Weirdly, I knew what he was going to show me and teach me and deep down I knew I wasn't ready. Before even calling him, I had this sense deep inside. I didn't hesitate and just went for it. Before parting he asked me, "What do you see?" I replied back, "Disks? But at a closer glance they are seals." He confirmed and told me that they were made of the Sacred Lunar fire from the depths of all Lunar regions. He added, "Our knowledge is vast, be ready when the right time comes. Record carefully."

Another time when I glanced over his name, I instantly saw a huge seal on fire but the flames were white and opened before my eyes. It blossomed like a flower but each petal was a seal and as it opened, it also fell off turning into dusts. Far away stood Etamrezh with one leg on top of a white lotus-like flower. The lotus petals were vibrating at a high rate whereas my body was shaking and my skin crawling. He was wearing a dark maroon suit with a white flower in the pocket square. His hair parted sideways in front, black and back white. His eyes were made of pure light and could sing. His hands clasped back. He was wearing black dress shoes. He took out a handkerchief from his right pocket and unfolded it in the air. Dust of tiny sparkles of light in pink came out and dispersed into the air. The air smelled so sweet which was very invigorating. The lotus he was standing on opened more and he pointed at me with his index to invite me in. My spirit easily left and went where he was and I stood on the lotus. Beneath us was a fountain of pure energy. As I watched, I noticed the energy twirling like a vortex sucking something upwards. There was this rush of energy pouring into my being that I can not describe. I saw terrains and mountains that I had never seen before. Each was a point, a seal. Not sealing anything in particular, but more like a gateway into that particular region. Permission must be granted before one travels there. Etamrezh grabbed me by my neck like a lion cub and descended to one of its points.

He said, "Here is gateway Aleph (in Aramaic). The purity of one's heart comes first. Thou shall not judge, only accept." I could hear a melody in my heart pouring out. I had never heard of that before nor had I known about its existence. Soon after the seal sang back a melody which vibrated, then nothing. Utter silence. All of a sudden, my entire head felt like an eye that stretched open wide like it was waking up from a long slumber, and during this transition, I could hear a faint screaming like a baby. Then this pure energy took over my entire being. Every orifice of my spirit felt so large and vibrating it felt like I was burning alive. Except it was not hot. It was not agonizing. It was actually liberating, yet there was the notion of pain attached to it. Out of nowhere, I found myself standing inside the lotus with Etamrezh watching the pool of vortex energy twirling. I looked at him in confusion and he said, "Child, the sacred Lunar fire can teach many things. However, one must be first able to face the ramifications of their actions of heart, mind and soul, before stepping into it. Most cannot comprehend nor carry the hefty burden they have created. We are the guardians of the Tabernacle. This Tabernacle is not of the Earth nor it is the ways of Yahweh. Tabernacles are many. This of which you just witnessed is one. Hidden within is sacred wisdom. Within each of you, there is a Tabernacle. Seek within and the doors shall open. Judge not, accept and go forth." He then put a ball of light into my heart and I was pulled away from the lotus. Etamrezh descended into the lotus and the flower closed off.

Warning

The Picatrix's talisman: Image of a man having two faces, with one facing forward and one facing behind.
Agrippa's talisman: A man with a double countenance, before and behind.
Bruno's image: Two men, one with his back turned, and the other looking forwards and gathering up his shaven hair nearby.

Black magic can turn **The House of Mastery of Life and Death** into the **House of Destruction**. Talismans of this spirit were traditionally made for the destruction of somebody. According to the Picatrix, Bectue wrath is helpful for the destruction and depopulation of a place and to separate wives from their proper husbands. Other old grimoires have also made it clear that he had a faculty to make women divorce their "just husbands."

When the Moon is in this position, it is definitely not a good time for anyone to argue with women, especially if they are married. With retrograde elements of the Moon, the black magician can make a woman unfaithful and desert her husband.

22ND GENIUS – RIVATIM

Arabian Name: Geliel
Western Tradition: Geliel
The Picatrix's Talisman: It was either not given or the text about it was destroyed
Agrippa's Talisman: A man with wings on his feet, bearing a helmet on his head
Bruno's Image: A helmeted man, flying with winged feet, returning safely
Rivatim is the head of the 22nd Mansion: Sadahacha, Zodeboluch or Zandeldena
House of Time and Space: 0°0'0 - 12°51'26" Capricorn
Position of the 22nd Mansion in the Moon Zone: Bordering the Mercury Zone

Rivatim is the fastest and most Mercurial of all important Lunar spirits. He is a great teacher of both the Moon and Mercury magic. This genius is a master of time and space and one of the best teachers of astral and mental projections in the Moon Zone. He looks like Hermes and he is sometimes called Mercury from the Moon. Rivatim is one of the greatest psychopomps too.

This spirit is famed as one of the most marvellous healers from the Moon. He helps with fast recovery from an illness. He boosts enthusiasm and sound thinking. Ask Rivatim for help if you observe psychopathological tendencies with people around you before they do something harmful!

Rivatim can help with anything you want to do fast. He was traditionally asked for help to make captives escape. You can ask him for help if you want to escape from a dangerous or undesirable situation.

Rivatim would be your best teacher if you are both attracted to the Moon and Mercury. The Moon is closest to Mercury in his region. He helps in all Mercurial matters, so if you are connected to any job which is under the influence of this planet (communication, art, diplomacy, literature, etc), you can ask him to be your guardian. Rivatim has, however, no reputation to be helpful in the financial sector, so if that is your concern, ask other people for help.

This spirit is one of the most important guardians of travellers. He grants fast journeys. If coming on time is your concern, ask Rivatim for help.

Rivatim teaches the magician about different ways of travelling to the Moon from the Earth (or other planets). If you want he may guide you in your journeys to the Moon and beyond.

Rivatim can show you how to use a magnitude of ways to reach Yesod through the Tree of Life. Many doors, tunnels, windows and gates serve both as blockades and portals to Yesod, so ask Rivatim to show you where to go and what to do if you are not sure. But you may also rely on your own intuition, consciousness and orientation. Of course, you will previously need to learn the glyph of the Tree of Life well, as this should help you choose your way wisely once you find yourself within the Tree of Life for real. The more experienced magician may visit Yesod, after visiting Chokmah, Geburah or any other sephirot before.

Rivatim can also teach you how to meet any spirit during your astral projection. The sigil of the spirit you want to evoke should be in the triangle and when you are out of the body, you may see it in your astral hand. With the more combined attributes, the more certainty, you would reach your wished destination. For example, if you like to meet Rivatim on the Moon, order yourself to go there by determining to state: "Shaddai El Chai, Yesod, 22nd Lunar Mansion, Rivatim!" You will start mental wandering and your consciousness will guide you there. Your physical body will be on the Earth while your consciousness is travelling to the Moon. During that journey, your astral body will capture in itself all necessary Lunar qualities in order to be able to be on the Moon at all. At the end of that journey, you will land on the Moon with your Lunar astral body.

It is common knowledge that the Sun would kill if you closely approach it with your physical body. But it will also kill if you go there with your Lunar, Venusian or Saturnian body. The only way you can enjoy walking on the Sun is if you go there in your Solar body. Following the same principle, you will be in your Martian, Venusian, Jovial, Saturnine, Solar or Mercurial bodies when you visit each of those named planets respectively. You cannot take a walk on the Moon in your Solar body, nor is it possible for you to walk on Jupiter in your Mercurial body. The transformation of one body into another goes naturally during your mental travels, and you will not usually pay attention to it. Maybe it really does not matter if you pay attention to it or not. Maybe you should just relax and enjoy, but that is not wisdom. Ask Rivatim to teach you if you want to understand and also master one day the process of transformation of your body into Lunar, Martian, Venusian or any other kind of planetary body during your mental travels!

We all have been taught that it is impossible to fly, but Rivatim may teach the experienced magician not only about this skill but also how to walk upon the water, rise into the air, etc.

Rivatim is a master of time and space, in which he closely cooperates with Dirilisin (23° Cancer), a head of the Earth Zone. Rivatim teaches the magician about orientation on the Moon, which is different from the Earth. He helps the magician to prolong or slow down the time. If you are in a good mood and busy doing interesting things, Rivatim may make your time run slower. If you are bored with your job or company, Rivatim may make your hours run like minutes. Your time will run differently compared to other people, which can be very helpful if you want to hide from somebody, especially if your life is in danger. You are unlikely to be ever late again with Rivatim as your protector.

As a master of time, Rivatim can also teach you about all mysteries of Monday and Lunar hours and how to properly use them in order to achieve your plans and goals.

Additional Observations Relevant to Rivatim's Teachings about Flying to the Moon

The Moon is approximately 384.400 km far away from the Earth. The journey to the Moon, if supposedly taken by train, at a speed of 200 km/h, would take 81 days. The flight to the Moon in the astral body takes about 10 minutes, but this is not the most convenient way to travel there. Even if you happen to be excellent at astral projections, your mind would likely bring you back to the Earth before you would reach the Moon. Robert Bruce, an expert in astral projections, says that it is possible to reach the Moon in a few seconds. And really, if you go through special cosmic channels from Malkuth to Yesod, the flight to the Moon cannot take longer than a few seconds. This tunnel is usually coloured light blue in modern glyphs of the Tree of Life.

Additional Observations Relevant to Rivatim's Teachings about Monday

Our ancestors noticed that the Moon is the most powerful on Monday, for which reasons Monday is called "the Day of the Moon" in English, German, French and many other languages.

Monday has a watery nature and is good for clairvoyance, talking to spirits, love spells, invisibility, working with the water element, journeys, home, family, medicine, cooking and dreams. Monday is also "Enochian Sabbath," because John Dee and Edward Kelley received the largest number of angelic messages that day. In the Middle Ages, the happiest days in a week were considered: Monday, Wednesday, Thursday and Sunday. Monday is also associated with Yesod and Archangel Gabriel. The Moon is the most active on Monday during its 1st, 8th, 15th and 22nd magical hour, which are all called the "Moon hours" of Monday. All other days also have their own Moon hours, but they are differently placed. For instance, when you perform the Moon magic on Saturday, you should choose its 7th, 14th and 21st magical hours; and on Friday you should choose its 3rd, 10th, 17th and 24th hours. The magician who follows the magical hours knows with more certainty than others, when exactly different planetary influences and energies are due to happen. With such knowledge, you would be also more confident with your plans and certain that they will bring good results. By consulting your magical calendar you would be in a better position to use all of the good things related to the Moon such as a safe journey, peace at home, harmony in the family, friendship, harvest, trade, health, self-confidence, intuition, lucidity and clairvoyance.

Evocation Experiences

Talerman

As I was getting closer to the Moon, my flight through space was getting more harmonious and enjoyable, and while I was flying, I was also hearing mystical cosmic melodies, which were so Divine that they might only be described by someone who also might happen to be a great composer. As I was concerned that my mind might interrupt my flight before I would reach the Moon, I stopped somewhere in the middle of the way to think about what to do next. I could see the Moon very clearly, but it was also obvious that I would not be able to reach it if I continue my flight. Then I stopped moving. While I was floating in space, I started meditating and after a while, I gave an order to myself, "Go to Rivatim!"

My mental wandering started instantly and my consciousness guided me to the Moon within a few seconds. There I met Rivatim who gave me incredibly much information about the Moon and showed me his library which was packed with a lot of ancient books. There were some old newspapers in his hands dated from the time before Christ. He told me to have a look. The article was about a woman who had been kidnapped while resting in a park somewhere in Babylon. He told me that spirits of the Earth and Moon zones had recorded daily news several thousands of years ago in form of newspapers and journals. All ancient newspapers are now available and could be read and studied at Rivatim's library, but also in many other libraries around the Earth Zone which are guarded by relevant heads.

While I was on the Moon, Rivatim also helped me meet there my late history teacher who was a friend of mine. At the end, Rivatim revealed to me that some people were planning a plot against me and that some magicians were going to betray me. Then he said that he would like to show me something which is so sacred that only a few people had seen it, but at the very next moment, I was regrettably already back on Earth.

The return trip to the Earth is usually immediate, safe and rarely uncomfortable, but it is also often followed by a sense of sorrow when it is over. My first thinking was that there cannot be anything faster in the Universe than coming back after experiencing an astral or mental projection.

KADILIYA

Dreaming is different when a spirit is involved. Sometimes things just do not work out the way you want. I heard Rivatim's voice telling me, "Go into the space of your heart and start from there". I felt like I could fall asleep but in vain. More distracting thoughts came. Then he said, "Go and engage with your thoughts. That way they won't have a strong influence in your dreamland." Finally, I fell asleep.

I dreamed of being in the kitchen at my current house. My landlord, his children and his wife were there too. The landlord was asking me weird questions like, "What does being a psychic mean?" I thought something was wrong. I looked around and saw his kids playing and his wife washing dishes. Things were completely flipped, which I had never seen happen before. My dream world was half of a circle which had never realized its other half. And I was inside the other half where I had never been before. Everything might have seemed somewhat normal, but the vibration was completely different. All my senses were extremely active. I lucid dream a lot and a lot of my works revolve around the dreamworld, but this was a different scale of lucidity that bypasses everything else. It might sound like a normal lucid dream, but believe me, it wasn't!

I said to myself, "This isn't real, none of this is real. Why do I feel like being flipped over? Why do I feel like I haven't been to this side of my dream world? What is this strange feeling?" Then I walked to the guest room. It turned out to be my childhood bedroom. I was at the window looking out. There were lots of letters. I took a letter to read while telling myself to remember it as it might be important. But it did not seem so. What if the whole dream was important? Being this aware could make me wake up, so I decided to try not to alter anything and see where this would lead.

All of a sudden, I took a bus and came to a very old town. The bus came to its last stop and I jumped off. I looked around.

It was windy and dusty. I saw a big Tibetan shop. Two women were working in the shop, one young and the other middle-aged. I walked around. There were statues and paintings of Ganesh. I greeted Ganesh because I thought perhaps this was his shop. The middle-aged lady came up and looked at me curiously and at first a little hesitantly, but then she smiled. I didn't even know why, but I was humming "Om mani Padme hum". She put her hand on my shoulder and spoke gently, "Oh! You know this mantra?" I nodded, and she turned to the younger woman and said, "She knows this, she's different from others. She's not here just to shop. She has a very kind heart." Their native language was Tibetan, but it was an old dialect. She asked, "Do you know what you want?" I said, "No, not yet. But I'm here for a reason." Then she replied, "Don't rush. Look around. You will find it". She asked where I was from and I said, "Far away, I'm from far far away if you know what I mean." I sensed they had never met a human before. The young woman wrapped up a gift to me and said, "Please, you don't have to pay. This is a gift from us. Thank you for coming from a such far distance. You are really far away from home. Travel safe and thank you for visiting our humble store." I took the gift, thanked them and left.

I don't know how, but I was all of a sudden standing inside a building which looked like a hospital. I walked around hoping that I didn't alter my dream. I could sense that certain parts of my brain were lighting up as if I was somewhere very deep in the subconscious. I also felt someone's hand gently resting on the top of my brain. I suddenly realized that as long as this hand was there, I could continue with my journey and that I would not wake up. I murmured to myself "Rivatim." I walked around and saw mini-marts. I was on a sudden mission to find talcum powder. I kept thinking about why I was looking for it when something happened. I saw again the middle-aged lady from the Tibetan shop walk past and I was about to tell something, but she turned, smiled and said, "We sold our store after your visit. We sold it for $18. It was a good decision. We realized it was holding us back from many things and creating a false sense of need. Now we are free from it all, thank you!", and she left. I couldn't believe they had sold that big store for $18?! Maybe she meant $18,000, as that sounded more right. But it was not dollars that mattered, but rather the number adding up to 9.

I started to investigate why I was on a talcum powder mission. The more I looked for it the more I realized it was for my mum. She was at the hospital, but what for? I kept searching for answers until I came to a room. A cousin of mine greeted me and asked, "Hey! You wanna see this? You wanna see your birth?!" I was stunned. She played a video on a small square TV. I watched my mum pushing in pain and a little baby came out. The baby was crying. She seemed very clean. I noticed the baby was levitating and heard my mum saying, "You were different from the first day you were born." I couldn't believe how small I was. The doctors put me in my mum's arms and she cried. Her tears seemed like diamonds. She seemed full of joy. Then the tape was over. My cousin pulled out the cassette. I asked, "Can I have this? Or buy this? What's the way for me to have this?" She said, "I don't know. This is a records room, I am not sure if you can take this. Maybe if you ask the person in charge of this place?" I walked out feeling a little down knowing that I could not take this with me. But I had seen it and it was good enough. My talcum powder mission was over. All of a sudden all the mini marts opened and sold talcum powder, but I didn't need it anymore. Now I was looking for my mum. I saw another cousin of mine inside her room. He was the childhood version of himself. I went in and greeted him, but something was not right. My cousin was asking me, "Is this how you spell angel?" But he wrote it as "angle", so I corrected him. Then his dad walked in, and the discussion about how to spell this and some other words continued. I knew that I would not find my mum. She might be in a room somewhere, but she was actually not here. There were just memories. There was no concept of time here. It seemed like it was happening right at that moment, but it was merely tapping into something that had already taken place. I thanked Revitim for showing me all of this. I may not truly understand it, but I appreciated the change in my dream world - this complete flip of sense and time. As I said, it had never happened to me before. It is really strange to leave the physical body, the astral body and the mental body and then penetrate through veils which are on another set of dimensions. I felt the hand is removed, and I instantly woke up.

Warning

Black magic can turn the **House of Time and Space** into the **House of Confusion.** According to the Picatrix, Geliel wrathfully is helpful for the binding of tongues, putting discord between two people, and making servants flee.

A magician may get tempted by using retrograde movements of the Moon to: lead other people astray, block their ways, confuse their minds, make them miscalculate, make them late, and obstruct their work and plans.

When you are late or lost, just remember to ask Rivatim for help.

23ʳᴅ Genius – Liteviche

Arabian Name: Zequebin
Western Tradition: Requiel
Liteviche is the Head of 22nd Mansion: Zabadola or Zobrach
House of Power : 12°51'26"- 25°42'52" Capricorn
Position of the 23rd Mansion in the Moon Zone: Bordering Mars
Talismans and Images: Traditionally used for malevolent purposes, they are presented in the 'Warning' section of this entry

Liteviche is one the most powerful heads of the Moon Zone. This spirit may appear in three or more forms. Liteviche is both an individual and a collective, with the dominant male aspect. All aspects of this spirit are very strong. They are among the best teachers of Martian magic from the Moon. Liteviche's region of the Moon is a bordering zone towards Mars. Many of their subordinate spirits are closely attached to Mars. Liteviche's zones are fiery parts of the Moon. In cabalistic terms, they are called "Atziluth of Yesod". He can guide the magician safely through all the parts of the Moon which are under his supervision.

Besides two other Lunar genii (Emvatibe and Emzhom), Liteviche can give very powerful banning formulae which the magician, however, is only allowed to use in some very urgent and dangerous situations. Liteviche's banning formulae are for taming wild nature and bad weather, while the formulae of the other two genii are mostly against malevolent people and spirits. The magician may use Liteviche's formulae to paralyze, confuse and prevent all actions of elemental forces that may bring harm to people. Liteviche may help with preventing the greatest earthquakes and the most disastrous tsunamis, and stop the wildest windstorms and volcanic eruptions.

Liteviche is also a great healer. He promotes healthy lifestyles and an optimistic and positive view of life. Liteviche is also one of the most important teachers of sexual magic on the Moon.

Finally, Liteviche was traditionally useful to bring friends together and for captives to escape and flee prisons.

Evocation Experiences

Talerman

I had an interesting but very short time with Liteviche on the Moon. I took a boat trip with him sailing through a silver lake which was so dense that you could freely take a walk on it. During our journey, he did not talk much. When I wanted something to say, he told me to relax and enjoy the scenery of the silvery-purple sky. When we arrived on the beach there I saw a group of very beautiful and intelligent people. Among them, a special girl, turned around to ask me if I was ready to follow her home. Maybe she was seducing me, and I said yes, but then the session was over.

ҠADILIYA

My experience with him was very strong. It began with me hearing the sound "Om" chant in my room. I noticed a change in the room. The atmosphere changed completely. A veil was opened and the spirit came through in his physical appearance. We went into a discussion about how and why words carry power. It is the intention and energy you put into them which brings them to life. If properly used, they can be very powerful. Most people do not know how to use them. We went through YHVH. By vibrating it, you are slowly bringing it to life. When I did so, I felt the electricity going through my body. He told me to vibrate IEHIEH and I felt intense heat which made me sweat instantly. Then I vibrated Shaddai El Chai and I felt the heat, but my sweat was cold, and I felt a breeze. So, you actually do not vibrate the names using your voice. You use your inner strength, will and light to bring it to life.

At some point, I realized I was about to fall into a deep sleep, so I did. I had a weird dream. I saw Liteviche, but he approached me in a sexual manner. However, I rejected him. He seemed very nice, gentle and fun, but doing anything sexual with him was strange to me. I felt like I was not learning anything, so I dismissed him while apologizing and left the dream realm.

Something disturbing woke me up. I heard loud heavy metal music going off on my phone and I got up to turn it off. But everything felt super eerie. I kept hearing a water drop sound in the room, but this sound had already been in my dreams in the background before. Now it was echoing in the bedroom. I felt something was off. I felt fear creeping into my heart slowly, but I told myself, "Hold on, I just woke up. But why does it feel like I'm still in a dream? Did something follow me to this realm?" The sound of the water drop slowly faded, and so did my worry, but I looked at my phone again not only it was on silent night mode but the last music I played was meditation music, and the only heavy music I had was called, "System of a Down," which is not considered heavy metal. What I heard was something else. It sounded like a loud roaring scratchy sound. The atmosphere in my bedroom was strange like a portal was opened and the two worlds were in one. Similar feelings like in Geburah, but colder and wetter. I eventually got up and cleared the room until I felt the portal was shut. It was hard to go back to sleep after that.

Warning

The Picatrix's talisman: A cat having a dog's head.
Agrippa's talisman: A cat having a dog's head.
Bruno's talisman: A cat with a dog's head, or a dog with the back of a cat, digging up the ground, and a man falling to the ground.

Black magic can turn the **House of Power** into the **House of Devastation.** According to the Picatrix, Zaadebola's wrath brings destruction and devastation, drives people from a place, destroys buildings, and divides husbands from their wives.

Magicians should not practice banning formulae driven by mere curiosity, but only when it is necessary. Some malevolent magicians might be tempted to misuse Liteviche's banning formulae to provoke the suffering of innocent people. According to Franz Bardon, Liteviche's powerful formulae may win wars and kill whole armies. Bardon underlines, as usual, that the magician with high ethical standards will "never dare to misuse the words of power that he has been taught."

Liteviche may make one very powerful, both physically and psychologically, but in the end, there is also a risk for such a person to become too proud, narcissistic, arrogant and aggressive.

24ᵗʰ Genius – Zhevekiyev

Arabian Name: Abrine
Western Tradition: Abrinael
The Picatrix's Talisman: The horn of a ram which is best and most apt. The figure of a woman with her son in her arms breastfeeding him is in it
Agrippa's Talisman: A woman breastfeeding her son
Bruno's Image: A woman feeding her son who has seized the horn of a ram which a large flock follows
Zhevekiyev is the head of the 24th Mansion: Sadabath or Chadezoad (Happy Star)
House of Alchemy: 25°42'52" Capricorn - 8°34'28" Aquarius
Position of the 24ᵗʰ Mansion in the Moon Zone: Towards the Jupiter and Saturn zones

Zhevekiyev is a male spirit that appears as a well-dressed gentleman. He has silver eyes with a hint of blue, a long chin and nicely combed hair. He is very friendly and entertaining and has a great sense of humour. He can be an excellent friend to the magician.

Zhevekieyev was traditionally asked for help with multiplying herds of cattle. He helps with agriculture. The modern astrologer Christopher Warnock says that this is a Mansion of nurture and nutrition. This can be taken literally, like the arrival of a new baby, but also may mean that the needs and desires will be fulfilled. According to Agrippa, this Mansion is good for married people. Zhevekiyev is actually one of the strongest protectors of marriages, and the families which are protected by him are characterized by their strength, solidity, stability and unity. This spirit is a great supporter of financially secure, strong, influential and powerful families.

Zhevekiyev also teaches about the power of faith. This genius encourages magicians to maintain strong faith in times of crisis. As one of the most recognized professors of ethics and cardinal virtues in the Moon Zone, he is advocating the restoration of harmony through morality and teaching about the beauty of equilibrium and normalcy. Zhevekiyev inspires the magician to treat other people with honour. He can tell the magician many interesting things about spiritual knowledge and gnostic movements in the Moon Zone.

Franz Bardon views Zhevekieyev's faculties at an entirely new level. According to him, Zhevekiyev teaches the magician about the question of life and death on the Moon. Zhevekiyev may show the magician Lunar graveyards and training centres whose mission is to prepare Lunar spirits for their future existence on the Earth, Mars, Venus or some other planets. Before reaching certain advancements, some of them must leave their lunar bodies behind, which is similar to our death on Earth. Thereafter, having become advanced spirits, they would be able to come back to the Moon if that is their wish or mission, but as they are also free spirits, they would be actually free to go wherever they want in the Universe and visit any planet or star.

Franz Bardon also recognized Zhevekiyev as the best alchemist of the Moon Zone. In that respect, Zhevekiyev's help is most efficient to those magicians who are also alchemists. He holds keys to all alchemical secrets from the Moon. If you successfully evoke Zhevekiyev, you can also request from him the proper alchemical key for you, but whether you will get it or not, will only depend on your maturity level. You may ask Zhevekiyev to show you his alchemical laboratory. Just a few people have had that rare opportunity to see Zhevekiyev and his subordinate spirits in their alchemical work. They use blood in alchemical operations to create concoctions against all kinds of diseases, even against the ones still regarded as incurable. In Zhevekiyev lagoratory, the magician can also watch the effects of four different temperatures for the four different grades of Great Work. Through that process, the magician can watch them create the final alchemical goal - Rebis, a substance which is also known as the most exalted quicksilver, and philosophical androgen. Zhevekiyev may further teach the magician about similarities and differences between Lunar alchemy and the alchemy which is used in the Earth Zone. Zhevekiyev and his subordinate spirits may reveal to the magician some of the deepest secrets of Yin principle in alchemy. For instance, they can explain in great detail why it is correct to regard silver as a genuine metal of the Moon.

Zhevekiyev can help you become victorious in all aspects of life (in which he is similar to Eneye, the head of the 8th Mansion of the Moon). For example, thanks to Zhevekiyev, you may become the most excellent artist on the stage. If that is your goal, your performances will be outstanding and the public will adore you. Even if you make mistakes, people will forget about your embarrassing moments, because Zhevekiyev has the power to erase anything potentially compromising from people's memories.

Zhevekiyev is able to help one achieve a high-level political position (president, prime minister, minister, senator, etc). If a high-level official causes harm to magicians, Zhevakiyev will be able to protect them and also punish that dignitary properly (more on that in the "Warning" section).

Like Emcheba, the head of the 13th lunar Mansion, Zhevekiyev is also a master of eternal health, youth and beauty. As one of the main initiators of mummial magic, Zhevekiyev helps the magician look young and have youthful energy even at an old age. Deceiving to the eyes, many Zhevekiyev's subordinate spirits look like children, but you should know that they are most likely not. They usually are in fact adults and ancients. If the magician sees a Lunar spirit that looks like a child, it is a big chance that it is one of Zhevekiyev's subordinates.

Additional Observations Relevant to Zhevekiyev's Teachings on Child-Like Moon Spirits

Swedenborg has emphasized in "Arcana Caelestia" and "Earths of Cosmos" that some Lunar spirits are very small. They are mighty spirits even if they look like seven-year-old boys. They have voices like thunder and their words come from their stomach (what it means Swedenborg knows). One lunar spirit told Swedenborg that they talk like thunders to scare evil spirits. The Austrian musician Jakob Lorber (1800-1864) has also said that some types of Lunar spirits look like children six or seven years old. Donald De Gracio, a modern author on astral projections, also saw adult Lunar spirits that looked like small children.

Evocation Experiences

Talerman

Zhevakiyev appeared in my triangle as an etheric figure soon after my conjuration. The whole ritual lasted for some three hours, though it seemed to me like it took not more than 20 minutes. The most important thing I saw was some incredibly small people playing in one of Zhevakiyev's playgrounds. Some of them were much smaller than thumbs. I had never seen such small intelligent humanoid beings before. And after I ended my session, they were still visible for a few seconds in their physical forms on my pillow and then they slowly vanished in the air.

Zhevakiyev also confirmed to me that friendly relations between magicians and "kings" have always been an important field of his influences.

He also showed me his laboratory where I saw radioactivity at work and some other very odd phenomena. He said that radio-active elements may be beneficial in some parts of the Earth Zone and Moon Zone but have devastating effects somewhere else as it has in our part of the world. Then he showed me a stone made up of zinc, uranium and quicksilver. He said that it is a healing stone on the Moon, but a deadly weapon in the material world.

By the end of the ritual, I saw many ships sailing on the ocean towards the coast of Zhevekiyev's Mansion carrying to safety sailors and other people who had drowned.

KADILIYA

The vision started with red curtains opening. A lean and tall man with silvery-bluish eyes walked on the stage. He was wearing a top hat and holding a cane. He had a giant smile on his face. He almost looked like a caricature. He didn't speak, but only used gestures. First, on the stage, there was a fish tank with water in it. He added things to it and the water changed colours. Then he thought for a moment and added something dusty and crumbly. Then he stirred it. All of a sudden, the whole theatre changed to a milky way and I heard people cheering amazed. He bowed and thanked them. Then he looked for a volunteer and he pointed at me. I looked around to make sure it was me, but there was no one else there to my surprise. What happened to the cheering I had heard earlier? I walked to the stage feeling very nervous. He put me inside a tall narrow cubical object that was my size and he closed the curtain. Then the whole thing started moving. At first, it felt like it was spinning, then going up and down, and finally stopping. A window popped out with a screen that said:

"Welcome to Zheyekiyev's magickal cubical! Please answer the question and select an option below. Whom would you like to see?

    1. (Dead relative's name, I can't say, an important one)
    2. Dead pet
    3. Your future
    4. Yourself"

I selected the number 4 and suddenly all the walls around me popped out. There were lots of cheering, sparkles and balloons flying around. I heard a lot of claps and someone yelling "Good choice!" Then I saw Zhevekiyev grabbing a small balloon and flying off. I also quickly grabbed one and went with him. I asked him for his name and he told me he was "Zhevekiyev." My introduction of myself was cut short because he claimed he knew who I was. He knew my name. He asked, "What can I do for you?" I told him about my yesterday early morning incident, and he confirmed that I was right about my suspicions about who had been behind it. I asked him about the dream I had that morning and he pointed me in a direction that was very useful. I asked him if there was anything he could teach me and he said, "One thing. Manifestation. It shouldn't be that difficult, but you are falling asleep and it seems you are in pain." He said, "Perhaps some other time, no rush. Oh, this is my stop, I'll see you later!" and he floated off.

WARNING

Black magic can turn the **House of Alchemy** into the **House of Violence.** Traditionally, Abrine's wrath was used to destroy the finances of allies and to prevent officials from doing their duties. The magician can ask this spirit to punish officials and politicians who abuse their powers. He can bring bad luck to kings, presidents, prime ministers, ministers and other dignitaries, and if they deserve it, he punishes them very badly.

Zhekeveyev may also bring the magician to his counter-genius' sphere where one may see some of the most violent aspects of the Moon, in which deadly fights are very common between gladiators, sportsmen, all other groups of people, and even children. Some of the most brutal and fundamental aspects of our world's religions come from this part of the Moon.

Counter-effects of this Mansion can cause all kinds of financial problems too. You can influence artists and celebrities to feel performance fright and even provoke rivalry and violence amongst peers.

25th Genius – Lavemezhu

Arabian Name: Aziel
Western Tradition: Aziel
The Picatrix's Talisman: A man cultivating his garden
Agrippa's Talisman: A man planting
Bruno's Image: A man planting a fig tree and another sowing corn
Lavemezhu is the head of the 25th Mansion: Sadalabra or Sadalachia
House of Plants: 8°34'28"- 21°25'17" Aquarius
Position of the 25th Mansion in the Moon Zone: Not specified
NB: There are three different spirits with the same Aziel:
- Aziel from the Moon mansion
- Aziel as a Shem angel
- Aziel as one of the seven Princes from the 6th and 7th Books of Moses together with: Marble, Ariel, Marble, Mephistophiles, Barbuel, Aziabel (or Aniquel).

Lavemezhu is often depicted as a shaman. In his human form, he looks like a chief from the Aztec time. In his non-human forms, he may appear as a plant with a face of a man or a plant with many faces. He is not very talkative. Rather than speaking, he likes to show his teachings by playing with a spectrum of colours, shapes and sounds. Lavemezhu's main faculty revolves around plant teachings.

Traditionally, this spirit helped with the protection of orchards and crops from accidents, and also with the preservation of trees and harvests. Franz Bardon saw Lavemzhu as a protector of the plant kingdom. This genius is one of the main guardians of our world's biosphere. He can demonstrate to people how to improve agriculture with the use of Moon magic and Lunar astrology. Lavemezhu can teach the magician how to turn whole fields of crops fertile by using cabalistic words.

Lavemezhu is one of the most significant guardians of all plants from the Earth Zone. Amongst all plants, he is especially fond of the ones that are connected to the Moon, such as lavender, camphor, white sandalwood, jasmine, ylang-ylang, iris, rosemary, narcissus, lily, poppy, eucalyptus, cabbage, lentil, beans, aloe, cucumber, pumpkin, gourd, carrot, mandrake, willow, linden, olive, and cocoa. This genius can help the magician make some of the greatest discoveries by comparative analysis of lunar and earth natures and while at it, he can present many opportunities for the magician to see the astral nature of the Moon with their own eyes. Thus the magician will gain extraordinary knowledge which could be of great contribution to natural science on Earth.

A large number of Lavemezhu's subordinate spirits play a crucial role in protecting and preserving plant kingdoms and life on our planet. He has billions of assistants on the Moon, Earth and space between planets. Each plant has its own guardian spirit that lives within itself and these spirits are free to roam around connecting with others in different environments. Each of these spirits carries great knowledge regarding the plant they reside in. Lavender spirits help to clear people's minds. Jasmine spirits and Narcissus spirits make people attractive. Iris spirits cure depression and give optimism. Poppy spirits enhance visions and dreams. Aloes and Eucalyptus spirits heal wounds, and burns, and prevent infections on injured skin.

Lavemezhu is also a special protector of mushrooms. The Mushroom spirits are known for their ancient wisdom. As they populate the Earth and the Moon since the immemorial time, they are a source of astonishing knowledge and wisdom. They have been working with adepts and highly spiritual people since the beginning of time teaching them how to tap into the subconscious mind to reach certain enlightenment. Lavemezhu and his subordinate spirits can also teach the magician how to prepare herbal medicines for treating various diseases and can help with loss of vital energy, strength and willpower.

This is a spirit of revival. He can offer great support if they would like to revive not only plants but anything in life such as love, friendships, ideas, hobbies, interests, happiness and reconnecting with the inner child. With him as the guarding angel, the magician will be able to resolve any problems promptly. Often after an evocation of this genius, the magician will feel inspired to reconnect with lost friends and family members. He can also inspire you to renovate your living space. Lavemezhu stands for some of the most optimistic aspects of the Moon. He is able to make the magician positive and happy. He is also a master of Feng Shui on the Moon, and as such he can help the magician create a happy home.

Like many other Lunar heads, Lavemezhu is a protector of travellers. However, according to tradition, he protects people who travel south and maybe it is because his powers are stronger there than in the three other cardinal directions. Traditionally it was also known that he helped with conveying messages and getting feedback quickly.

Additional Observations Relevant to Lavemezhu's Teachings on Agricultural Astrology

Plinius the Elder gave instructions on agricultural work based on the Moon phases. Some people still plant potatoes and other vegetables during the New Moon phase. Some women still breastfeed in accordance with lunar circles. Geruna Dunvich, a modern Wicca, plants on Monday if her purpose is growth; on Thursday if she wants to attract good luck; and on Friday during the Fool Moon to attract love and to give presents to her garden spirits.

Evocation Experiences

Talerman

I have always started all of my previous evocations of the angels of the Moon by conjuring them in the name of YHVH, Shaddhai El Chai and Archangel Gabriel, after which they would usually appear in my triangle in more or less visible forms, after which I would use different methods to deepen my conversations with them: though scrying, meditations, visions, astral and mental projections or lucid dreaming. Sometimes nothing would happen during the evocation, in which case they would usually later during the day or night appear to give me some spiritual insights and experiences.

During this evocation of Lavemezhu, I felt a very strong presence of him in my room, but I did not open my eyes nor speak to him because I somehow knew that he would be gone the moment I tried that. So, eventually, he was standing by my side for maybe an hour. He stood there and I sat here. While he was standing there in silence, I enjoyed the sound of waves and felt exactly as if I were on the beach. So, this is how it went on until he confirmed to me that he was a king of plants. That is when I thought I might finish my session when he showed me his castle on the Moon which looked like an ancient fortress. I saw plenty of children playing in front of its gates. Lavemezhu welcomed me into the castle. It had many large gardens, a botanical park with plants from the Moon and a zoo with Lunar lions and many other known and unknown animals.

During the next half of the evocation, it was raining outside, though there had been no sign of the rain before the evocation. I wondered if the evocation of Lavemezhu could influence the rain. I might experiment with this in future.

KADILIYA

It started with me seeing an African lady sitting alone on the ground singing. She was a little chubby, wearing flower-patterned clothes that were blue and white. Her voice was soft and gentle, but the music was coming from her heart. You could follow the vibration like a thread all the way down to her heart world. I went there following the vibration until I came to a place which I cannot describe. Then something in front of me started moving, and I went up close to take a good look at it. It was a plant that came out of the ground and completely opened itself. It was a sunflower, a little taller than me. It opened the bright light from its face facing up the skies. I didn't see anyone around but I wanted to see what the sunflower was looking at and why it was so bright, so I climbed up using its leaves.

When I made it to the top, I saw there was actually a row of sunflowers blossoming. They all had the same light coming out of their faces while facing the sky. I looked up and all I saw was light, but I also noticed myself shifting. It wasn't like I was flying or getting pulled up. It was a gentle float that you could hardly notice if you were not paying attention. Then I saw a door. Everything tilted back to normal and the door opened. I step through the door, and it was pitch black. I started to walk when I noticed some light, but it disappeared again.

Slowly around me, fluorescent mushrooms were lighting up. I heard a beat like drumming. I kept walking. All the plants around me lit up bright green and white and purple and blue. The ground beneath me was like a belt that was slowly moving. The beat and music became stronger. I felt like I was in a giant rainforest in the dark, while everything was alive, dancing, and the colours were just amazing. I wondered if this was like an acid trip. It was like a psychedelic painting. Then I could hear someone singing. The music reminded me of "Deep Forest". The path I was on lit up. It looked like something very familiar and all of a sudden I got overwhelmed with this emotion just like when I was on my mother's ayahuasca.

I came to a man I knew was Lavemezhu. In fact, I had already met him in Peru. Now I understood certain visions I had had back then. It was so groovy. I was very happy to meet him again. I cannot share my further experience after that because it is heavily linked to ayahuasca and it is sacred. It felt like my experience with ayahuasca never actually ended. In the end, I had the strong sense that I must go back and continue the rest of my journey with plant medicine. Then I came out and ended the session.

Warning

Black magic can turn the **House of Plants** into the **House of Annihilation.** According to tradition, Aziel wrath is used: to besiege cities and villages, to take enemies and do evil to them as much as one pleases, to separate wives from their husbands, to destroy harvests, to bind a man and wife or woman and her husband so they cannot copulate, to bind a part of the body so that it cannot function properly, and to strengthen the prison of captives.

The black magician can also use retrograde movements of the Moon to make people depressive or obsessive.

Franz Bardon has also pointed out that it is also possible for the magician to learn from Lavemezhu how to change whole fields of green into a desert. Needless to say, there also needs to be a good reason for such an action.

26ᵀᴴ Genius – Empebyn

Arabian Name: Tagriel
Western Tradition: Tagriel
The Picatrix's Talisman: The image of a woman with her hair unbound and in front of her a vessel placed as if to receive her hair
Agrippa's Talisman: A woman washing and combing her hair
Bruno's Image: A woman combing her washed hair, with a winged boy in front of her
Empebyn is the head of the 26th Mansion: Alpharg ili Phragal Moccasin
House of Stability: 21°25'17" Aquarius - 4°17'10" Pisces
Position of the 26ᵗʰ Mansion in the Moon Zone: Bordering the Sun Zone

Empebyn is adored by many spirits from the Moon. She is a beautiful female angel and one of the most gracious queens in our Universe. This genius is a true Solar angel of the Moon. She guards all secrets, subjects, mysteries and arts against the Moon Zone. Empebyn is one of the greatest teachers of both Lunar and Solar magic and she is also one of the best healers from the Moon Zone. She is also one of the guardians of agriculture, commerce, money matters, farming and gardening. First encounters with this spirit will typically take place in the dream realms.

Empebyn was traditionally evoked for love matters and to bind people in mutual love. She is also one of the guardians of marriages. Ask Empebyn for help if you need to find the right partner! If she has already agreed to help, especially when the Moon is in its 26th Mansion, know that your love adventure will most likely be a success.

Empebyn teaches about equilibrium and encourages people to refrain from exaggerations of any kind and relax while finding balance within themselves on all levels. She can help by showing the imbalances that are within one's heart and mind and by suggesting solutions through deep meditation, clearing rituals and even mantras.

Magicians may ask Empebyn to bless their homes. Any buildings which are under Empebyn's special protection will become practically indestructible because they will get the guarantee from this angel not to be destroyed by earthquake, fire, flood or any other kind of natural calamities.

Empebyn is even a guardian of good shopping, as she could grant the magician them to buy what is needed for a good price.

This genius is the guard of all travellers by land and air. Traditionally, when the Moon was in this Mansion, the best time to travel was in the morning. However, she was not favourable for ocean voyages.

Empebyn's teachings regarding densities are astonishing. There are many densities, but only 125 of them were ever talked about by the Archangel Metatron and mystery schools (especially those schools dating back to the ancient Egyptians). From the 1st to the 7th density is considered to be the First octave, and from the 8th density is a starting of a new octave. The higher the spirit evolves, the more polarization disappears. Empebyn shows that once magicians pass the Abyss on the Tree of Life, they will see and experience the disappearance of polarity. Advanced magicians who are allowed to stay on Tipharet, will also notice the disappearance of polarity. One of the best teachers in that subject is the Archangel Raphael of the Solar sphere. Talking about this topic, Embeyn once said, "One can only see from the mind that creates its own reality and only advanced magicians through much training are able to experience life outside of the Earth and the Moon."

Being the teacher of the Solar magic of the Moon, she explains how the Sun influences the mental, astral and physical plane of the Moon, life on the Earth and human bodies. She is a great cabalist. She may tell you many unknown and untold secrets about the mutual relations between Yesod and Tipharet. She has a huge region of the Moon that borders the Sun Zone.

The Sun is the main source of life in our part of the Universe and Empebyn's role is to transmute its power to generate life on the Earth. Her mission is essential for life on our planet, but she is also helped by all of her subordinate spirits.

Empebyn offers advanced knowledge about other Lunar bodies and natural satellites too. There are about 170 known natural satellites orbiting the planets in our Solar System, and Empebyn can introduce the magician to their heads and other relevant spirits. The magician may gain extraordinary knowledge from such encounters and may also be granted that rare opportunity to explore in his or her astral and mental bodies the realms of Ganymede, Callisto, Io, Europa, Titan, Trion, Phobos, Deimos, and other natural satellites.

Empebyn and her subordinate spirits may also reveal to the magician some of the biggest secrets about how the Moon and other natural satellites influence the Sun. They closely work with guardians of the Solar Gates whose mission is to bid farewell to all departing Solar spirits while welcoming all new inhabitants of the Sun. Empebyn teaches the magician how to reach the Solar level of consciousness. She is considered to be one of the best psychopomps to guide people and other spirits from the Moon to the Sun.

This genius closely cooperates with Ophaniel, the main representative of the Ophanim order. Often they can be seen together during one's astral journeys. Ophaniel is one of the most important angels and best teachers from the Moon. Cabalistic literature names him as one of the governors of the Moon and the most important angel of the Lunar Wheel.

Empebyn is also a guardian of all foundations. The stability of the Moon is her responsibility. If the foundation is not stable, its structure cannot last. Evoke Empebyn if you want your manifestations to last long, be stable, and have strong foundations. Empebyn and her spirits teach the magician about the foundation in the following subjects:

- Foundation of the Tree of Life;
- Foundation of the astral plane;
- Foundation of life;
- Foundation of one's personality and character;
- Foundation of a building, organization or state;
- Foundation of the magician's life (from early childhood).

Additional Observations Relevant to Empebyn's Teachings

Yesod: Yesod is the sum of the eight sephirot. It receives from them their forms of emanations and transfers them to Malkuth for their final materialization. The magician should apply the above principles and use the influences of Yesod to materialize their ideas. The idea which has been fully formed in Yesod is only one step away from its materialization on Earth. It can still be prevented, but only by dominant karmic reasons or some very powerful curses. Yesod is placed on the Pillar of Equilibrium, below Tipharet, and above Malkuth. It is the first reflection of Tipharet and the second reflection of Kether. As it has no lights of its own, Yesod is receiving the sunlight from Tipharet. The physical Moon is a dark celestial body. Since it has just a tiny atmosphere, sunlight cannot spread there and the lunar sky is left to be dark even when the Sun is shining. Yesod is at the base of the Tree of Life. It is written ISVD in Hebrew, which is a combination of two words: Yod and SVD (mystery). One of the secret names of Yesod is Mystery of Yod.

Foundations

The Moon is also seen as the foundation of the Indian tradition. The Indians think that the Moon is a foundation for a stable life. The magician who stands on the Moon's foundation has achieved full control over the four basic elements and also overall lunar phases, influences and energies.

Ophaniel

Ophaniel has 16 faces, 100 pairs of wings and 8,466 eyes. He has so many eyes because he is constantly watching God. According to the Books of Enoch, Ophaniel has 88 angels under his command. Their function is to move the Moon across the sky. Ophaniel is ranked below Galgaliel who rules the Sun. Some cabalists say that Ophaniel is Sandalphon's son. Ophaniel's sigil has the shape of the lunar wheel. The magician may evoke Ophaniel with this sigil, but may also use it to evoke some of his 88 subordinate spirits and angels. If the magician is interested in this subject and wants to learn more about the Ophanim order of the Moon, ask Empebyn for help.

Evocation Experiences

Talerman

My first evocation of Empebyn did not bring me more than a few interesting magical dreams, but I consider them to be important as they were full of Lunar symbolism such as water, rivers, travels, crabs, lobsters, fish, Scorpios, etc. Anyway, I have had a very nice and relaxed day and feel very positive vibrations after this evocation.

Kadiliya

I was invited to a place that had an amazing blue lagoon. The sky was baby pink with some golden shine to it, and the Moon was full and big. I was greeted by a blonde lady who looked like a model. Shortly after, she said, "I'd like to invite you to come to my place in Australia. Oh, you must come and see the fireworks from my place on New Year's Eve! Please, say that you will come! It will be a magnificent view". She then turned around to talk to other people. She was wearing a blue dress. This was Empebyn. I saw the opera house from where I was standing and I saw the fireworks. These all gave me the impression that I was seeing the near future. I started walking towards the fireworks and came to this blue lagoon. The water was so clear you could see the sand beneath it. I went in to feel the water and I saw two sharks swim up to me. They were black and white and long. I wasn't afraid. In fact, the sharks rubbed their faces on me briefly while circling around me.

I eventually got out of the water and got into a small red car and started to drive. The turn I took wasn't where I wanted to go, but the traffic took me in that direction, so I went with it. All the traffic took me to a beach. I parked my car at this parking lot where I always seem to park my car. Then I walked out and started to head to the beach. I laid down my towel and sat watching and listening to the waves. The waves were small, the colour of the ocean was blue, and the sky was pink with that same Full Moon. Soon after I was approached by an old friend from high school. We talked and he asked me to get coffee with him sometimes. I hesitated at first but ended up agreeing.

From afar, I saw two brothers. They are angels. They closely work with Archangel Metatron. I don't know their names, but when Metatron doesn't show up for whatever reason, these two usually come to me. I believe that they are very closely associated to the Earth Zone and get somewhat involved with human matters. They were watching me and giving me information that seemed faint to grasp. Then a bright light appeared and I woke up.

Warning

Black magic can turn the **House of Stability** into the **Destroyed House.** Traditionally, Tagriel wrath was used to make the incarceration of captives firm and to cause them evil.

Empebyn or her counter-genius can teach about Qlippa of Yesod and its relation to Qlippa of Tipharet. Qlippa of Yesod is ruled by Gamaliel (Polluted by God). It is usually connected to the act of creation whose goal is not a beautiful offshoot. This gives a possibility of the birth of monstrous beings and ideas.

The Sun may bring life or death depending on the level of its intensity, so the magician may also ask Empebyn or her counter-genius to teach them about all previous cosmic disasters caused by the Sun, which a few times in history have threatened to extinct life on our planet too.

Black magicians may be tempted to abuse Empebyn's knowledge in order to: shake the foundations of other peoples' manifestations; destroy buildings, roads, bridges, communications and infrastructures; and bring chaos amongst people, destabilize all countries, confuse governments, and ignite revolutions of enormous scale.

27th Genius – Emzhabe

Arabian Name: Abliemel
Western Tradition: Atheniel
Emzhabe is the head of 27th Mansion: Alchara or Alyhalgalmoad
House of Growth: 4°17'10" 17°8'36" Pisces
Position of the 27th Mansion in the Moon Zone: The earthly part of the Moon Zone
Talismans and Images: Presented in the 'Warning' section of this entry, since they were traditionally used for malevolent purposes

Emzhabe has a female form, but she is androgynous. She has orange wavy hair. Her presence is strong. Even if you do not see her during your evocation, your doors and windows are likely to move. For others, they will move for no apparent reason, but you will know that it is because of Emzhabe. Alongside the 1st genius and the 14th genius of the Moon, she is the best initiator into the Moon Zone. Franz Bardon has also conferred that this head is a "marvellous initiator into magic." As she is a universal philosopher and one of the best teachers from the Moon, with her help you will certainly improve your magical capabilities. The magician, who has not evoked any of the Lunar heads before, might find in Emzhabe the best option to start with.

She covers most of the subjects from the Moon Zone, but her focus is usually on growth. Traditionally, she was called to acquire profit and increase merchandise, unite allies, increase harvests, plant, sow, merry and heal illness. The Moon is one of the most changeable and the least static planet, and Emzhabe is responsible for its changes and growth. If you want to see your children grow healthily, ask Emzhabe to help! Furthermore, the magician may ask Emzhabe to help with all other matters, such as love, career, or finances. One can grow very fast as a magician in all possible directions with Emzhabe's help.

Emzhabe is the best teacher of the earth magic from the Moon in which she closely cooperates with the following heads of the Earth Zone whose faculty is the element of Earth: Nadele (24° Aries), Baalto (25° Taurus), Amia (18° Capricorn), Kamual (19° Capricorn) and Yromus (25° Aries).

This genius may introduce the magician to some of the most important kings and queens of fairies, nymphs, sylphs, gnomes and salamanders from the Moon Zone. All of those wonderful beings are, as Cabalists would say, "the expressers of the powers of Assiah of Yesod", which means that their special role is to protect nature and preserve the kingdom of minerals, plants and animals in the Moon Zone. They closely cooperate with the similar expressers of the powers of Assiah of Malkuth, whose role is to preserve life on Earth. One of Emzhabe's main tasks is to take care of minerals, oars, crystals and stones of the Moon and Earth zones.

Emzhabe might seem quite strict at the beginning, but she is a benevolent, patient and tolerant teacher. She dislikes laziness, but if you are hardworking and eager to learn, she would certainly accept you as her student. It is best to ask Emzhabe first for help if you have any basic questions about the Moon. The magician who is a beginner in Moon magic may find in Emzhabe one of the best spiritual guides for obtaining general knowledge about the Moon Zone. Emzhabe can also reveal to the magician many secrets about other Lunar genii. She can even teach you about their lessons on their behalf, which is important to know if you are not able to evoke other genii of the Moon for some reason.

Emzhabe Teaches the Basics of the Following Subjects

- 28 Lunar Mansions
- Yesod's inner Tree of Life
- Shaddai El Chai
- Archangel Gabriel
- Cherubim angelic order
- Clear Intelligence
- Lunar magical squares
- The Moon is the Major Arcana of the Tarot.
- The Moon in Enochian magic
- The 28th aethyr BAG
- Lunar stones and crystals

Additional Observations Relevant to Emzhabe's Teachings on Lunar Stones and Crystals

Moonstones

Ancient sages used moonstones for divination, amulets, and protection against epilepsy and madness. They also used them to approach Aphrodite and Selena. Travellers wore them for safe journeys and farmers placed them in their gardens for agricultural growth. Some magicians put a moonstone in their mouths to see the future. Moonstones diminish stress and help women give birth.

Pearls

Pearls are traditionally linked to the Moon magic, are a lunar symbol of water, woman and clarity, and are also a sign of angelic perfection which is not given, but rather taken through transmutation. Old Gnostics saw in a pearl the most valuable hidden essence of each person. In China, peals represent the yin principle. Pearl spirits enhance good judgment and promote mercy.

Crystal Quartz

Crystal quartz might be blue, green, pink, white or smoky. This crystal has been used for thousands of years in shamanistic rituals. The 14th Century European magicians often made their wands of quartz. Crystal quartz is also traditionally used in divination, to make pendulums efficient, and also for lucid dreams (for which reason people practised putting them under pillows in the 19th century).

Beryl

Beryl, another lunar stone, is carried against storms and drowning. This stone also provides protection against all other things and averts laziness. Emzhabe may teach you how to see the future and invoke the rain with beryl. The famous crystal which belonged to John Dee was made of beryl.

Additional Observations Relevant to Emzhabe's Teachings

Clear Intelligence

Its task is to purify emanations and numbers, approving them and correcting their designs before they would materialize on the Earth. Some cabalists call Clear Intelligence "the Machinery of the Universe." They also sometimes compare the Earth with a large ship and the Moon with the motor of that ship.

Magical Squares

They were used by: the Chinese (the River Map - 2000 years ago), Jews (patriarch Enoch), Indians, Arabians ("zaigreh") and Byzantines (scholar Manele Mascopulos). The colours of the Lunar Magical Square are opposite to the colours of the Solar Magical Square. The numbers in the Lunar Magical Square are often taken yellow with the background in purple. Use the Lunar Magical Square when you want to: construct Lunar talismans, evoke Lunar spirits, concentrate on solving problems, reach the adequate Lunar frequency for easier communication with Lunar spirits, and construct different symbols and sigils of the Moon Zone. The highest intelligence of the Moon according to the Lunar Magical Square is Malcha betharsithim hed beruah schehakim, which is responsible for all benevolent Lunar influences like friendship, satisfaction, luck, safe travel, multiplication of wealth and banishing evil. Numbers associated with the Moon are 9, 81, 369 and 3321 because:

- Each horizontal and vertical line contains 9 numbers;
- The square has a total of 81 numbers;
- The sum of each line is 369;
- All numbers summed up give the number 3321;

- All Divine names of the Moon have a numerical value of 9 or 81;
- The name of the Spirit of the Moon has a value of 369.

Four Main Planes of Yesod

The Moon we see in the sky is just a mundane chakra of Yesod. There are four main planes of Yesod:

- Y, H, V, H of the Moon;
- Assiah, Yetzirah, Briah and Atziluth of the Moon;
- Fire, Air, Water and Earth of the Moon;
- Spiritual (Akasha), Mental, Astral and Material/Etheric parts of the Moon.

The Moon in Tarot

It is the most profound cosmic Lunar energy responsible not only for the creation of our Moon but for all moon-like celestial bodies in our planetary system and also in the whole Universe.

The 28th Aethyr BAG

There are 30 aethyrs. They generally do not correspond to the 10 sephirot on the Tree of Life, except for the last 3 (TEX, RII and BAG), which are, though in their own rights, quite related to Malkuth and Yesod. Many magical aids and correspondences may facilitate the magician's contact with the sphere of BAG such as Lunar seals, Monday, while cloths, silver, camphor, amber, white sandalwood, willow, rosemary, jasmine, olive, quartz, shells, moonstones, Lunar amulets, Lunar talismans and theghbyui8989999kkkkk7yu7uu][number 9.

Evocation Experiences

Talerman

I evoked Emzhabe for the first time about five years ago. During that evocation, she gave me to read a list of the names and sigils of all the 28 Lunar angels. It was obviously the same list which had also been given to Franz Bardon.

Emzhabe also confirmed, because I had had some doubts about it, that the Moon genii from Franz Bardon's book are the same as the Picatrix's angels.

Kadiliya

I stood outside in my front yard in my pyjamas and stared at the Moon. A spirit came to me telling me she is the 27th spirit of the Lunar mansion and that her name is Emzhabe. Honestly, I didn't even get the chance to check who was next on my list. So I was a little surprised. I asked for her sigil and I was shown. This spirit was in a female form. However, she told me that she is more androgynous. She had that glare and look in her eyes which tells you to take her seriously. Emzhabe showed me how to use the lunar energy and draw it within myself. She told me why that was important and what it could be used for. She taught me how to break through my current reality via the Lunar magic, but that was only scratching the surface.

Her lesson gave me a great sense of adventure and thrill. The lesson was very powerful. I instantly used the skills she taught me in that moment to penetrate through some things that had been holding me back, things I had not understood. The instant I used them, they were effective. I gained a lot of understanding for myself. After she showed me and taught me a few things, she faded away. I thanked her.

This spirit teaches with delicate precision. She is in all seriousness focused on the subject. During her lesson if the person cannot focus or struggles to understand, she will find some other alternative ways to pass her knowledge through. I would say that she will leave, only if the person does not care about learning.

Warning

The Picatrix's talisman: The image of a winged man, holding in his hands a dish with a hole in it, and raising a bone to it.

Agrippa's talisman: A man winged, holding in his hand an empty and perforated vessel

Bruno's image: A winged man lowering an empty-holed flagon into a well.

Black magic can turn the **House of Growth** into the **House of Overgrowth**

Traditionally, Abliemel wrath was used to destroy: fountains, pits, medicinal waters, springs, wells and baths; abundance, and buildings. It was also used to: put travellers on the sea in peril, prolong the incarceration of captives, and do evil to whomever they wish. In order to prevent such calamities, the magician should use the Second Pentacle of the Moon which prevents malevolent Lunar spirits to cause: flooding, heavy rain, earthquake, hurricanes, tornadoes and other natural calamities. The hand in this pentacle is showing God's name El and the angel Abariel. A verse from Psalm 56:11 is written in the pentacle and it may also be used to prevent natural calamities.

By harming other people, the black magician may also be tempted to bring overflowed of luxuries and abundance in his or her own life.

Either Emzhabe or her counter-genius can introduce some basic secrets of Qlippa of Yesod. They can also teach the magician about all aspects of the reversed Moon in tarot. The black magician can also be tempted to use Lunar Magical Square for harmful purposes.

28ᵀᴴ Genius – Emzher

Arabian Name: Anuxi
Western Tradition: Amnixiel
The Picatrix's Talisman: A fish having a coloured spine on which is written the name of the lord of this Mansion
Agrippa's Talisman: A fish
Bruno's Image: A man throwing a golden fish into the water, and many fish swimming towards it.
Emzher is the head of 28th Mansion: Albotham or Alchalcy
House of Sympathy: 17°8'36" Pisces-0°0'0" Aries
Position of the 27ᵗʰ Mansion in the Moon Zone: Towards the Sun Zone

Emzher comes across as a male spirit. You may need to ask him to materialize if you want him to take a proper form. Otherwise, he might present himself as a golden crest on armour. Once materialized, he is described to have a sharp angular chin, square jaw, small lips and tall nose. The pupils of his eyes are half silver and half orange, and they look like fire. He has white long hair that is tied back. This spirit has a very calm and nurturing demeanour about him. His very diverse faculties in teachings are focused on: all aquatic-related topics, healing, temperature changes, Enochian magic, Moon magic, Solar magic, astrology, interpersonal relationships, marriages, all forms of travel, and protection.

Franz Bardon has mentioned that Emzher is one of the best teachers of the water element. This spirit is deeply connected to the water and all aquatic life forms for which reason he was traditionally called upon to help people gather all fish in one place for the fishery. If permission was granted him, all the fishermen had great results in obtaining fish. This genius can teach the mature magician how to master the art of water elements and their aquatic life. For the magician who seeks knowledge regarding aquatic life or underwater settlements on the Moon and the Earth, Emzher would be the perfect spirit to ask for help. Emzher can also guide you back into the past to show how the prehistoric people made their first ship vessels, but also to the future to give you an idea of how advanced ship technology will look like.

When it comes to healing, Emzher masters all forms of water healing and healing with temperatures such as hydrotherapy, medical magnetism, underwater massage, cryotherapy, floating, infrared saunas, saunas, hot stone massages and hot stone saunas, balneotherapy, thalassotherapy, and transferring life energy from one to another. If asked, Emzher may invite the magician to use spas and medicinal springs in the Moon Zone and to meet their guardians who can also share many secrets about water healing. Magicians should definitely ask Emzher to help them try some water from the Moon. With the help of Emzher, one can learn how to control atmospheric temperature and body temperature by will, which can be very useful in extreme weather conditions or in dangerous situations.

Emzher was also called for help to increase merchandise and harvests. His influences can be seen wherever there is serenity and tranquility where the earth bears fruit, fishing is good, the weather is nice and trade gives profit. This spirit helps with love affairs by creating deep connections with one another and also deep meaningful friendships.

The magician who has good relations with this head will learn how to be persistent. With the help of this angel, one will learn not to give up easily and strengthen their will to persist until one reaches their goal of success.

Emzher is also one of the guardians for travellers in which his speciality is to provide fast help when something goes wrong with the journey.

Emzher is one of the greatest astrologers of the Moon Zone. Ask him for help, if you have a hard time understanding Chinese and Indian Lunar astrology and their interpretations of the 28 Lunar Mansions. Emzher can help with calculating Lunar mansions, days, phases and other hidden aspects of Lunar astrology.

Emzher's specialities are not only related to Lunar magic, but also to Solar magic. She can guide the magician from the Lunar regions to the Solar regions and show the rest of the pathways to all other sephiroth. If magicians are hesitant to go from one zone to another due to fear of the unknown, they can evoke Emzher to personally guide them or to introduce them to the gatekeepers of other regions of the Tree of Life.

Emzher is a great angel to call for help if you want to meet some of the following orders of the Lunar spirits:

- Cherubim
- Lavanim
- Yerahim
- Enochian Lunar angels
- Angels of the Moon from cabalist tradition
- Olympic spirits
- Lunar spirits from Solomonic tradition

In conclusion, as the last of the 28 Lunar genii, Emzher gives the last instructions and lessons about Lunar magic and Moon Zone. Whatever remains to be understood and complete, spirits from the Moon come to him for advice and final lessons.

Additional Observations Relevant to Emzher's Teachings

The water of the Moon

The Bulgarian mystic Omraam Michael Aivanhov has said that Yesod's water is the foundation of the wisdom of all other sephirot, so he advised his students to drink it up when they would reach the Moon. Chinese alchemists connected the Moon to the elixir of immortality. The Moon-water is mentioned in Vedic tradition as divine nectar – soma (also called the Drop of the Golden Light in the Sky, Creator of the Night, Bringer of the Snow, Head of the Brahmans and Husband of Nakshatri). Indians say that the Moon pours soma into plants and that it is a master of flora and its growth. Indian gods also drink soma as a drink of immortality.

Lunar Zodiac

The Lunar zodiac of 28 Lunar Mansions has been used in China since ancient times. Each of the Chinese 28 Lunar Mansions has its own guardians in a shape of an animal. On the other hand, ancient Indian astrologers used a system of 27 or 28 Lunar Mansions - Nakshatra – which were connected to Indian gods. Medieval Arab and European astrologers usually calculated the position of the Moon in the sky using the tropic zodiac in the frame of fixed stars. Chinese astrologers traditionally calculated the position of the Moon in the sky by the days in a week, starting with the first Mansion which always falls on Thursday, and most often on the first Thursday of each month. Western and Eastern people counted stars and constellations differently and watched the sky with different eyes. Indians looked at the sky in their own special ways too, but their system is closer to the Arabian and the Western tradition than to the Chinese. The Western, Indian and Chinese Lunar

Mansions do not match at the same time (on 16th December 2011, the Moon was in its 12th Western Mansion, 10th Indian Mansion and 16th Chinese Mansion). Positions of the Moon mansions are today calculated with software programs, which makes calculations very easy but less magical. Explore Western, Chinese and Indian Lunar astrology separately from each other! Draw conclusions about what they have in common at the end when you need to conclude your divination (not at the very beginning as many would do)! Both Lunar and Solar zodiacs should be used equally. So was done by Michael Scott, a court astrologer of Fredrick II (13th century), who wrote in *Liber Introductorius Maior in Astrologiam* that astrology is the "wisdom in man" received from both the Sun (which gives wisdom) and the Moon (which gives knowledge about good and evil).

Protection During Travelling

The Third Pentacle of the Moon is good for that purpose. Many Christian travellers use the icon of St. Nicolas, the protector of travellers and seamen. When the journey gets hazardous, one may also recite the verse from Psalm 40:13. Many old gods were protectors of safe journeys and the magician should evoke them according to their own tradition.

Cherubim

Emzher may introduce magicians to the Cherubim, the angels of light and glory (in old Assyrian "karabu" means "mighty"; and in old Acadian "kuribu" is to be "blessed"). And most often he will introduce the magician to Kerubiel (the leader of the Cherubim according to Zohar) and some of his subordinate spirits (like Zaral and Jael). The Cherubim are the guardians of many things and places such as: palaces and temples (like in old Assyria and Babylon); the Tree of Life in the

Garden of Eden (Genesis 3:24), the Ark of the Covenant (the Second Moses Book 25:18), fixed stars (according to Pseudo-Dionysius) and Akashic records (according to some authors). Cherubim are charioteers of the Divine chariots, holders of the Divine thrones and transmitters of Divine consciousness to all physical manifestations. They were seen in Babylonia as high-winged spirits with lion or human heads and bodies of different animals. This picture of the Cherubim was later taken by the Jews and Christians. In the Book of Ezekiel (10:14), the cherubim have four faces representing - lion, ox, human and eagle. St. John describes them as divine animals with six pairs of wings and many eyes. The Third Book of Enoch tells that they have four faces, four wings and 2000 thrones. Talmud associates them with the chorus of the blessed animals, but according to the Christian dogma, they are of the second chorus of the first angelic order, whereby they are the first ones below the Seraphim. The Jewish cabalist Moses Maimonides positions them to the ninth angelic order.

Lavanim and Yerahim

Emzher also initiates adepts to the angelic orders of Lavanim and Yerahim. Those two angelic orders are very similar to each other and both are also closely related to the Cherubim. The difference of their name is due to the two different ways of telling the Moon in Hebrew (Yerahim comes from "Yerrah" and Levanim from "Levanah"). Further on, Emzher may introduce the adept to Yahriel (the main angel of the Yerahim) and Levanael (the main angel of Levanim). Levanael is a male, and Yahriel is a female angel. When Levanael is evoked, three vertical lines can be drawn as it is the symbol of the Levanim order. Yahriel on the other hand is one of the most important and beloved female angels of the Moon. Not only did she endure a lot to help many Lunar spirits to find their paths, but she also inspires the compassion of many other Lunar spirits towards humans.

Enochian Lunar Angels

Some Enochian magicians are fond of evoking Levanael since his name is written on Sigil Dei Aemeth, as one of the seven angels of Heptarchy (or the angels of seven celestial circles). They regard Levanael as the angel of the lunar celestial circle and some of them consider him to be the "first in secret knowledge." Emzher may also introduce the magician to Carmara, an important lunar angel whom Donald Tyson calls "King of the Kings of the Moon". Some other important Enochian lunar angels are:

- Alndood, the third of the six seniors on the Watchtower of Fire;
- Htnorda, the third of the six seniors on the Watchtower of Air;
- Lavazrp, the third of the six seniors on the Watchtower of Water;
- Lzinopo, the third of the six seniors on the Watchtower of Earth.

The Enochian magician Benjamin Row paid special attention in his *A Book of the Seniors* to the Lunar senior Lzinopo, a female spirit. She appeared to him in a long blue-purple dress. She had a crown on her head with the shape of the Waxing Moon. She looked like the English queen Elisabeth I. Lzinopo introduced herself as "Goddess Lzinopo, the senior on the Enochian Watchtower of Earth". She told him that her name means: "The First who came from the Deep" or "The first in Lower Waters". She explained to Row the lunar currents of the Earth, the combination of "lunar flexibility" and "earthly power and stability" gives "peace and silence," which are the two basic virtues of the earth element.

A few Angels from the Cabalist Tradition

- Elimiah is one of the most important angels of the Moon. The core of his name is "elim," which might be translated as "gods," "holy," "celestial beings" or "sons of God" (Psalm 29:1). Elimiel is a ruler of the tides and a guardian of the travellers and the explorers. His sigil consists of the Waxing Moon crescent and the Hebrew letter Kaph.
- Iaqwiel is a very powerful angel of the Moon, but it seems that just a few magicians have ever even tried to evoke him.
- Arkan (Arhan) rules over the lower rays of the Moon. He is a king of angels of the air, sylphs, Monday and the Western wind (alternatively called Wind of the Moon). Bilet, Missabu and Abuhaza are his ministers (called "arcan rex") and they: award the magician silver; transfer things from one place to another; give speed to the horses, and discover secrets of all people. They can also help the magician understand the mysteries of Yesod and help him in orientation during his astral or mental wanderings on the Moon.

The magician may conjure them this way:

Conjuro et confirmo super vos angeli fortes et boni, in nomine ADONAY, ADONAY, ADONAY, EIE, EIE, EIE, CADOS, CADOS, CADOS, ACHIM, ACHIM, IA, IA, Fortis, IA, qui apparavis monte Sinai, cum glorificatione regis ADONAY, SADAY, ZEBAOTH, ANATHAY, YA, YA, YA, MARINATA, ABIM, IEIA, qui maria creavit, stagna et omnes aquas in secundo die, quasdam super coelos, et quasdam in terra. Sigillavit mare in alto nomine suo, et terminum, quem sibi posuit, non præteribit: et per nomina angelorum, qui dominantur in primo exercitu, qui servient ORPHANIEL angelo magno, precioso et honorato: et per nomen stellæ, quæ est LUNA: et per nomina prædicta, super te conjuro, scilicet GABRIEL, qui es præpositus diei Lunæ secundo, quod pro me labores et adimpleas, &c. ut in conjuratione diei Dominicæ.

Lunar Spirits Mentioned in Solomonic Tradition

Yashiel, Shioel, Vaola, Vehiel, Abariel, Aub, Vevafel, Jahel, Sofiel, Jahadiel and Azare.

Olympic Spirits

Aratron, Bethor, Phaleg, Och, Hagith, Ophiel and Phul. They share among themselves 196 cosmic provinces and full control over one of the 7 planets. They give their special names to the magician who might use them in the next 40 years. They were first mentioned during the Renaissance and later in Arbatel -1655 - and a few other grimoires. The Olympic spirit of the Moon is Phul. She is a female spirit, appearing often as a hunter, with a green tunic or a dress of purple colour, silver armour, a hamlet and a bow in her left hand. Her face is of a warrior, quite pale but beautiful. She has been seen riding a white-winged ox. She rules over 7 cosmic provinces and controls the waters of the Earth and is a master of the undines. Phul is capable of destroying evil spirits of the water and curing illnesses caused by the negative lunar effects. She also transforms every metal into silver and teaches the magician to make extremely powerful silver talismans. She helps in astral projections. It is best to evoke her on Monday with her special sigil (easily available in many books).

Evocation Experiences

Talerman

Thanks to Emzher, I have seen many different orders of the Moon Zone. In October 2009, I decided to accept his advice, so when I reached the Moon, a beautiful lunar female spirit offered me to drink a glass of Yesod's water. She took another glass for herself. We cheered and drank it up. I have never in my life tasted anything so subtle, tasty and strange. I saw her again while I was writing this book. She said that her name is Woman in 'Silver' and 'Scarlet Colour.' She is one of the Emzher's subordinate spirits. She told me: "When you taste Yesod's water, you also nourish yourself with the best quality of water from all other sephirot". She confirmed to me that Yesod is the foundation upon which the whole structure of the Tree of Life is based, containing essential substances of all other sephirot.

While I was writing this book, one night, I connected to Phul through Emzher. Phul asked me to follow her to one of her seven cosmic provinces. There I had a chance to swim in a yellow river, watch trees (whose beauty seemed to be eternal to me) and entertain with her beautiful undines. There I also saw my older son who later told me that he had dreamed that same night about catching a golden fish from a silver river. The same night my younger son dreamed about being in the Sun. As the "King of the Sun," as he was called in that dream, he was watching with his binoculars from the Sun what was happening down on the Earth. After that experience, when I dream the same dreams with my sons, I would take it as a sign of our joint connection to Phul.

Through Emzher, I have so far also seen a few Enochian Lunar angels and Lunar gods and other spirits from different traditions.

KADILIYA

It started with me seeing a golden chest armour shining before my eyes. Then the rest became a man, he took my hand and there we stood in front of a road. I asked for his name and sigil and he confirmed that he was Emzher. I asked where we were, and he told me "Route 22." I asked 'Why?" He replied, "This is the path that connects all paths. Now, where do you want to go? The path before us takes us to Tiphareth, to our right that is Netzach and to our left it is Hod. Which one do you want to see the most?"

I looked at all three paths and at first, I felt nothing. I thought about Netzach, but I knew I would be going there anyway and I was not very drawn to Hod, so I looked at Tiphareth and I felt warmth. Emzher said, "I see You're looking at the path to the Sun, does it feel familiar?" And it did. I had felt this before. I went a little deeper and realized it was the same feeling in my heart space. I asked, "So, there I will meet my higher self and spirit guides, huh?" He smiled and replied, "Ah yes. So you know, as you should. If we go there right now you will meet everyone, hopefully". But I thought to myself I was not ready. So I said to Emzher, "No, I'll go there eventually, not right now though". He smiled and said, "Very well. But before we go I want you to do something for me. Go ahead and put one foot a step ahead, and leave the other one where it is now". I didn't think too much of it and did what he had said, but felt nothing. He continued, "I want you to feel the ground beneath your feet and connect to it." I followed his instructions and all of a sudden I felt the texture of the ground. The foot I put in front felt soft and the one behind felt little rough. I connected to the energy and I felt the strong energy of the Sun and the Moon. The difference was within that one little step that divides all.

Part of me really wanted to go to check out Tipharet, but I held myself back because I just felt that the timing was not right. We took the road behind us and we came to a place that looked like the ocean. We talked a lot about the subconscious mind and how to start making changes there. He gave me many tips. He also gave me some information about my health which was really great, and also how to heal myself. I felt this spirit closely connected to the Sun as well as the Moon.

Warning

Black magic can turn the **House of Sympathy** into the **House of Hate.** Anuxi wrath was traditionally used to: besiege cities, get rid of things, destroy an area, make treasures lost, make incarceration of captives firm, and inflict horror on sailors on the sea.

Emzhabe knows how to constrain his counter-genius and should be evoked any time the magician would notice that Lunar influences cause: flooding, hurricanes, heavy rains and all other problems with water.

The magician should also use the Second Pentacle of the Moon which prevents Lunar spirits to cause: earthquakes, typhoons, tornadoes and other natural calamities. The hand in this pentacle is showing to God's name El and the angel Abariel. A verse from Psalm 56:11 is written in the pentacle and it may also be used to prevent natural calamities.

Call Emzher for help when lovers and friends start questioning, discrediting and mistrusting each other. He is also very helpful against thirst, dangerous undines, astral larvae, parasites, sea monsters and all other possible bad aspects of water. Call this angel to prevent sailing vessel disasters.

Black magicians may be tempted to abuse knowledge received by Emzher to pollute and intoxicate water and the atmosphere and to cause all kinds of infectious diseases. They may get assistance from many different kinds of sublunar demons to bring destruction and spread negative Lunar influences around the Earth in many different ways too.

www.ingramcontent.com/pod-product-compliance
Lightning Source LLC
Chambersburg PA
CBHW060021100426
42740CB00010B/1549